JOURNAL OF WASHINGTON IRVING, 1828

JOURNAL OF WASHINGTON IRVING

1828

AND MISCELLANEOUS NOTES ON
MOORISH LEGEND AND HISTORY

Edited by STANLEY T. WILLIAMS

NEW YORK

AMERICAN BOOK COMPANY

MCMXXXVII

MADE IN U.S.A.

CONTENTS

INTRODUCTION   ix

JOURNAL   1

MISCELLANEOUS NOTES ON MOORISH LEGEND
  AND HISTORY   69

v

245053

ILLUSTRATIONS

MAP   *facing page*   1

FACSIMILES OF IRVING'S SKETCHES

   IRVING'S SKETCH OF A PORTION OF THE ALHAMBRA *facing page* 20

   IRVING'S SKETCH OF THE "SUSPIRO DEL MORO"   "   "   34

   IRVING'S SKETCH OF A CASTLE   "   "   44

   IRVING'S SKETCH OF A TOWN AND VEGA   "   "   46

INTRODUCTION

Here in the bright southern sunlight, within view of the very villages and ranges traversed by Washington Irving one hundred and eight years ago, I have lingered too long over the pages of this dim, old Journal. For this excess of interest in Irving's thirty-seven days' pilgrimage through Castile and Andalusia, I must plead several unpersuasive reasons. One of these is the daily presence, as I write, of the blue Mediterranean and of the white-capped ridges of Granada. These have lent a kind of reality or factitious importance, in my study of the Journal, to Irving's constant allusions to such scenery. Another is my antiquarian curiosity in following exactly his route from Granada to Málaga, and from Málaga to Ronda, on the roads themselves and also on the maps stored away in the dusty quiet of the Biblioteca de la Sociedad Económica,[1] in the Plaza de la Constitución. And, as a final sentimental excuse, I have struggled long with this document because I now write for the last time (a blessed boon to my friends!) on Irving's Spanish exile.

Such moods are certainly too personal to motivate a book which aims to add a scholarly mite to our

1. This library contains four editions of books written by Irving, two in English, two in Spanish.

knowledge of Irving's life, as a supplement to the Spanish chapters in my recent biography.[1] This is a more valid reason, namely, that this Journal from March 1 to April 6, 1828 (discovered in Ohio after I had searched for it during many months in Spain!), fills conclusively a lacuna in Irving's first Spanish sojourn (1826–1829). Mr. George S. Hellman's printing of Irving's Journal[2] for 1826 and 1827 told the story of the composition of the *Columbus,* and Miss Clara Louisa Penney's later volume[3] dealt chiefly with Irving's stay in Seville. From May 1, 1827 to March 1, 1828 no complete Journal is yet available,[4] but Miss Penney's edition of the Journal of 1828 continued the tale of Irving's travel, showing him at Gibraltar with the Spragues, at Puerto de Santa María with Böhl von Faber, and at Seville with Fernán Caballero.

Just prior to this record there fits neatly, almost to the very hour, the present Journal. If the other Journals deserve publication, even more does this manuscript, for, besides furnishing a missing connec-

1. See Chaps. XIII, XIV, XV.
2. See *The Journals of Washington Irving,* ed. W. P. Trent and G. S. Hellman, Boston, 1919, February 10, 1826–April 30, 1827.
3. *Washington Irving, Diary, Spain, 1828–1829,* ed. C. L. Penney, New York, 1926, April 7, 1828 February 28, 1829.
4. Portions of this missing Journal of 1827 were quoted by P.M.I., II, 267–271. For Irving's last Spanish Journal, See *The Journals of Washington Irving (op. cit.),* III, 64–100.

tion in the Spanish Journals, it reflects Irving's *first*
stay in Granada, and also his meticulous note-taking
in the mountains and on the seaboard where Moor
and Christian fought so bitterly. Of the five weeks
reflected in the new Journal we already know much
from letters, but we are unfamiliar with Irving's im-
mediate impressions as, after the weary two years'
study in Madrid, he first saw Moorish Cordova and
the Alhambra. Indifferent in ancient Málaga to its
nineteenth-century political heresies, he wandered
in the courts of the Gibralfaro and looked down in
imagination upon the Christian hosts relentlessly
driving the chieftains from their earthly paradise.
In this acropolis of Málaga he meditated not on the
opposition to Ferdinand VII but on Al-Makhari,
here "where the weed and wild flower mingle &
grass grows over the crumbling tower." [1]

Therefore, without ascribing to it either literary

---

1. See in the present work, p. 54. It was characteristic of Irving
that in this, as in his other Spanish Journals, he was silent concerning
the contemporary political disturbances, which so deeply interested
him after his return to this country in 1842. His concern was with the
Moorish past, which he studied in preparation for *The Conquest of
Granada* (1829) and *The Alhambra* (1832). Notes for both these books
were now in his luggage. But in the various "*pronunciamientos*" or
disturbances such as that of Torrijos, three years later, Irving
was not interested. See F. Guillén Robles, *Historia de Málaga y Su
Provincia* . . . Málaga, 1874, pp. 637–694; and *Apuntes Históricos de la
Reconquista de Málaga* . . . Málaga, 1887, pp. 35–36.

or unusual biographical importance, I have committed this Journal to a full printing, primarily because it rounds out Irving's story. In addition, as suggested in the first paragraph of this Introduction, I am convinced that lovers of Andalusia will enjoy it. Such will, perhaps, be amused to perceive how few essential changes have occurred in this savage, beautiful region since Irving's day. Robbers and *contrabandistas* have vanished, and, near the precipices where Irving clung to his *burro*, the *Malagueño* driver, vociferous and smoking a casual cigarette, steers his huge automobile, with the death-defying agility of a mountain goat, around the hairpin turns of modern roads. Yet here are the fig trees and the olive trees, here the deep ravines and the lofty, snow-crested heights, and, especially, here in these mountains still dwells the eternal Spanish peasant, greeting you, as when Irving knew him, with his courteous *"Dios le guarde!"*

The Journal, moreover, is informative concerning a problem which has long interested a few special students. Whence came Irving's material for those tales which have been so many times translated into Spanish as the *Cuentos de la Alhambra?* [1] Partly, of course, from books; the Journal adds one or two

1. See S. T. Williams and M. A. Edge, *A Bibliography of the Writings of Washington Irving, A Check List*, New York, 1936, pp. 33–35.

new titles [1] of sources for *The Alhambra* and *The Conquest of Granada*. But these two books derived also, as this Journal demonstrates, from legends bequeathed by Irving's devoted *Granadino*, Mateo Ximénez.[2] Whatever Irving heard from this loquacious "*hijo de la Alhambra*" he embroidered from his reading, but parts of the tales took form from anecdotes which he jotted down from the lips of Mateo. A comparison of the Miscellaneous Notes on Moorish Legend and History [3] will hint at the provenience of the romantic tales which so charmed England and America a century ago.

This Journal is the property of Mr. W. T. H. Howe, of New York City, and Cincinnati, Ohio, whose generosity, so well known to students of American literature, has made possible its publication. Bound in half-roan, 12mo, it is five and seven-eighths inches in length and three and seven-eighths inches in breadth. Written in both ink and pencil, it bears on its front cover a label with the figure "19" (apparently the number in the series of Irving's Journals), and the words: "1828 March 1. to April 7." Irving, owning a modest talent in drawing, illustrated this Journal. It contains eighteen drawings, of

1. See in the present work pp. 78, 80.
2. See in the present work, p. 21, and *The Alhambra, passim.*
3. See in the present work, pp. 67–80.

varying distinctness, four of which have been repro-
duced in the present book.[1] The location of each of
these sketches, and of blank and torn pages, has been
indicated in the notes.

The figures in brackets show the pagination (sup-
plied by the editor) of the Journal. The manuscript
has proved very difficult to decipher, and almost
certainly there have resulted errors in transcription,
but at this final reading few actual blanks remain.
The attempt to make a precise record of Irving's
route [2] has been hampered by the fact that some of
the small villages which he mentions are no longer,
apparently, surviving, but in the main every place
of importance which he visited has been identified.
The erasure or the illegibility of a single word has
been indicated by a long dash (——); of two words
by two long dashes (—— ——); of more than two
words by two long dashes and a note (—— ——[1]).
In so far as possible the manuscript has been repro-
duced exactly as Irving wrote it, including errors in
punctuation, spelling, and capitalization. Abbrevi-
ated references occur in the notes to *The Works of
Washington Irving*, Riverside Edition, New York,
1864–1869; P. M. Irving, *The Life and Letters of
Washington Irving*, New York, 1862–1864 (P.M.I.);

1. See illustrations facing pp. 20, 34, 44, 46.
2. See map facing page 1.

and S. T. Williams, *The Life of Washington Irving*, New York, 1935 (S.T.W.).

For assistance in the preparation of this Journal I am indebted to Mr. Stanley T. Bush, of Torremolinos, Spain; Miss Ruth Hall, of New Haven; the Librarian of the Biblioteca de la Sociedad Económica, Málaga; Señor Enrique Tolosa Ortega, of Granada; Mr. George Graves, of Málaga; and, in particular, to Mr. Robert F. McNerney, Jr., of Yale University.

STANLEY T. WILLIAMS

Torremolinos, Málaga, Spain
1 March, 1936

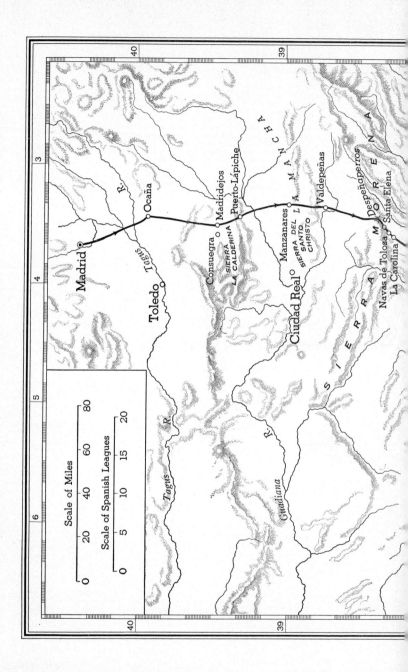

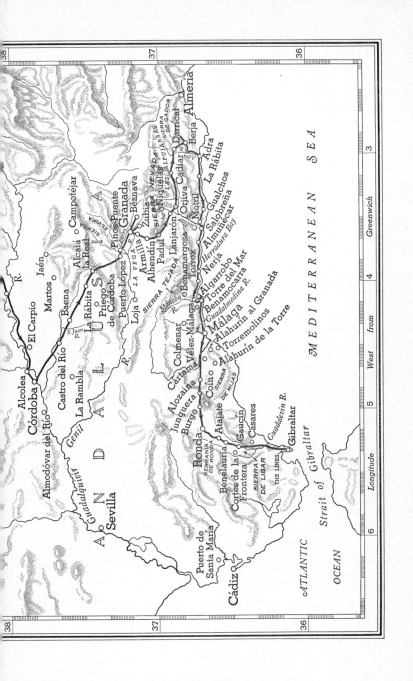

JOURNAL

[1] [1] 1828. March 1.

at 12 oclock take leave of Peter [2] & Theodore [3] at the coach office and set off in the Diligence for Cordova in company with Mr Gessler, Russian consul general & Mr Stoffregen [4] Secretary of the Russian Embassy – Beautiful sunny weather. Trees about Madrid just budding forth – almond trees along the canal in blossom. Diligence travels at rapid rate 2 leagues an hour – Arrive towards sun

1. Preceding the regular entries of the Journal, notes occur on the inside of the front cover, and on the leaf opposite (really the fly-leaf of the Journal). Then follows a blank page (the back of the flyleaf), and on the following page (right) the Journal begins, p. [1]. These notes read as follows: " D Pedro Laborde Calle del Mar Malaga La Ripa Corona Real del Pirineo Huerta Anales de Galicia Mora Hist de Toledo See the Chronica de los Principes de Asturias y Cantabria (P Irving chez Mòns Meyer Aven St Martin Rouen) [flyleaf:] my lodgings at Madrid at the house of Fermina Rodriguez No 9— Plazuela St Cruz quarto principal.) Madrid Francisco Saledo y Espejo de Turon the acquaintance of Cadiar Pedro Antonio de Trevilla Bishop of Cordova —— [eleven illegible words] The moorish spies quick to catch him—"
2. Peter Irving (October 30, 1772–June 27, 1838), Irving's devoted older brother, who, after a brief career as a physician and journalist in New York society, passed the latter part of his life in Europe. See S.T.W., Index.
3. Theodore Irving (March 9, 1809–1880), the third son of Ebenezer Irving, Washington Irving's brother. See S.T.W., I, 327–328.
4. For descriptions of Gessler and Stoffregen, see P.M.I., II, 285–286, 303.

set at Ocaña [1] little town situated on a hill with
small green valley below it – good hotel – at supper
we have a lively Catalonian – who talks in rapture
of Andalusia – As to La Mancha he says it is poor
because the inhabitants are not spurred to labour by
their wants. They [2] can live upon almost nothing –
They scarce want any clothing and are content with
hovels – a country where of ten men two work but all
the ten eat.

Sit round Brasero [2] after supper with the conduct-
or of the diligence & talk of robbers [3] – The guard
of the diligence has been captain of a band but
pardoned thro the intercession of the Bishop of Jaca.

Leave Ocana at 12 oclock at night – We have two
guards on horseback – Brown cloaks – guns & sabres
– full moon – wild dreary open country

[3] 2 [March]. Morning early – one of the great
plains of La Mancha – reddish earth ridge of hills
to south – Moon sinking behind hills in east – sun
about to rise – Castle of Consuegra [4] to the right –
on a ridge of Hill – Castle large & square – looking

1. Ocaña, a town in the province of Toledo, is southeast of
Aranjuez.
2. A pan of live coals used for heating rooms.
3. A favorite theme of Irving's in his letters from Spain. See S.T.W.,
Chap. XIII, note 105.
4. On the crest of a hill overlooking the town of Consuegra are
the ruins of a castle, said to have been built on the foundations of a
fortress of the period of Trajan.

over the great plain – Stop to Breakfast at Madre-
dejo [1] at 6 oclock in the morn[in]g within a league
of Consuegra [2] and in sight of the blue Hills at the
foot of which is Puertolapiche [3] where Don Quixote
was knighted

at Madrejeo[?] [4] – diligence drives under roof – great
Hall – or barracks – two deep arches open to Kitchen
– fire on ground smoke rises thro cone

[4] Pass through puerto a Lapiche where Don
Quixote was knighted – We are joined by Polinario –
formerly Robber at present guide – good physiog-
nomy –

Pass through Manzanares [5] near which Slidell [6]
was robbed. Polinario tells me that Caruco[?] was
dead –

Country begins to improve – Vines & olives The

1. Madridejos, a town with about seven thousand inhabitants in
the province of Toledo, is approximately sixty miles distant from
the city of Toledo.
2. A town of about eight thousand inhabitants in the province of
Toledo, a few miles to the west of Madridejos.
3. Puerto-Lápiche, a town in the northwestern part of the province
of Ciudad Real, in the eastern foothills of the Sierra La Calderina.
In the early years of the nineteenth century this town was merely a
group of inns.
4. I have been unable to locate a place of this name. This may be
Irving's second misspelling of Madridejos.
5. A town of about fourteen thousand inhabitants in the western
part of the province of Ciudad Real.
6. Alexander Slidell Mackenzie (1803–1848), American naval officer. See S.T.W., I, 468–469, 476–477.

Spaniards say plant vines for the children & olives for the grandchildren –

Hills – Sierra del Santo Christo [1] arrive at 3 oclock at Val de Penas [2] – Houses of this part country clay built – men wrapped in brown cloaks small monteras [3] – all collected in the great Square –

call to see wine Establish[t] [5] of Marquis S[t] Cruz – old woman goes to call superintendant – children bring chairs to gate – they dance for us

3[d] March

at Midnight we leave Val de penas Fine Moonlight – mountains silvered with dew – two guards on horse back passing like shadows – Silver Brook glittering in moonshine – Dark masses of mountain contrasted with gleams of moon shine – Despena de perros [4] – rough precipices – look like towers with men on them – arrive at St Helena [5] – country begins to soften – Distant view of Snowy Mountains [6] – German Settlements traces of countenance & language – at S[t]

1. Part of the Sierra Morena near Valdepeñas.
2. Valdepeñas, a town of about twenty-three thousand inhabitants, in the southern part of the province of Ciudad Real.
3. Cloth caps.
4. Despeñaperros, one of the most famous mountain passes in the Sierra Morena between Castile and Andalusia.
5. Santa Elena, a town of about three thousand inhabitants in the northern part of the province of Jaén.
6. It is possible that Irving could see from the slopes of the Sierra Morena the snow-capped peaks of the Sierra Nevada, although these were some seventy-five miles distant to the south.

Helena we buy [6] Silver coins of the times of the
Moors – probably since the battle of Navas of Tolosa [1] – Pass in sight of castle of Navas [2] & thro village of Navas of Tolosa [3] – broken country aloes
begin to appear – arrive & breakfast at Carolina [4] –
Hedges of aloes – Bear leader with his bear & mon-
key – From Carolina there is a beautiful avenue of
trees – country begins to be pleasant – improves as
we advance – Hedges of aloes – country covered with
olive trees – air mild –

[7] at 3 oclock arrive at Andujar [5] – neat little town
– clean houses – patios – a house with balcony or
rather atelier at the top – Court yard & court
with trophies of the chase – Heads of deer – wild
boars – wolves &c – Take an evening walk to the
Guadalquivir with Gessler & Stoffregen cross the

1. Irving refers to "La batalla de las Navas de Tolosa," one of the
most memorable conflicts in Spanish history, in which the Spaniards,
led by Alfonzo VIII, King of Castile, turned back and routed the
Almohad Arabs, on July 16, 1212. Research by scholars has demon-
strated that this battle actually took place about seven miles to the
north of Navas de Tolosa between Santa Elena and Miranda del Rey.
2. Near the town of Navas de Tolosa.
3. Navas de Tolosa, a town in the northern part of the province
of Jaén.
4. La Carolina, a town of about eight thousand inhabitants, in the
province of Jaén, on the southern slope of the Sierra Morena.
5. Andújar, with a population of about sixteen thousand inhabitants, is in the province of Jaén, and on a plain, to the right of the
Guadalquivir River. For Irving's description of Andújar in a letter,
see P.M.I., II, 287.

bridge where Dupont [1] fought – Air soft, balmy & delicious – beautiful landscape – little court yard at the Hotel before the dining room with citron & orange trees full of fruit

[8] Leave Andujar at midnight – drive thro naked country weather overcast

March 4 – at ½ past 6 – change horses at Inn below Carpio [2] – the latter situated on a swelling hill dominated by an huge square tower of red stone in ruins – Commands extensive view – deep bend of the Guadalquivir – Hills covered with olives in the distance – castle of Carpio [3] the scene of battles between moors and christs – belongs to Duke of Berwick – country rather naked –

cross the Bridge of Arcola [4] built of marble – level – with many arches. See Cordova at distance –

1. When in 1808 a French army under the leadership of General Dupont occupied Andújar, the town was almost completely abandoned by its inhabitants, and was subsequently sacked by the French. Here in 1809 Joseph Bonaparte and Marshall Soult established general headquarters.

2. El Carpio, in the province of Cordova, with about twenty-five hundred inhabitants, has an Arab tower dating from the year 1325. This is probably Irving's "huge square tower."

3. The "castillo del Carpio" was built in 1215 by García Mendoza de Sotomayor.

4. Irving refers to the famous Puente de Alcolea over the Guadalquivir River, near the village of Alcolea and about six miles from Cordova. This bridge is important in the history of nineteenth-century Spain for its associations with two battles, one on June 7, 1808, and another on September 28, 1868. In the former a small Spanish

nothing imposing in the approach – Hedges of aloes
& Indian fig – trees in young leaf – arrive ½ past 9
– put up [9] [1] at Hotel of the dilligence – very bad
[12] cathedral – patio with oranges ascend the tower
– rich plain by which Pelistes [2] escaped – ascended
a gorge of the mountain –
rich level carpeted plain toward south with Almodovar [3] towering on a promontory in the distance
Huerta del rey Almanzor [4] a beautiful grove, in the
vega [5]

---

army engaged a French force greatly superior in numbers, and in the
latter rebel troops under General Serrano fought the loyal army of
Isabella II.

1. This page contains only this single line of writing and a sketch,
apparently of the Puerta de Almodóvar, one of the gates in the
Moorish walls of Cordova, leading to the Paseo de la Victoria. The
sketch, very faint, bears the inscription: "Almodovar del rey."   On
page [10] Irving drew a sketch called "cabeza del Rey" or "cabeza
del Pez" and added: "Hills with convents – country houses dotted
with olives rich plain at foot of mountains." Page [11] he devoted
to a sketch of a plain, a river, and a tower. He resumed his Journal
on page [12].

2. See "Legend of the Subjugation of Spain," *Spanish Papers*, 132–
145.

3. The town of Almodóvar del Río, with about four thousand inhabitants, is fifteen miles distant from Cordova. On the right bank
of the Guadalquivir River and on the eastern side of a high hill, it
is famous for its castle, with a high, detached tower.

4. Almanzor (939–1002), one of the most famous of the Arab
chieftains in Spain, helped to establish the fame of Cordova, his
capital, as a seat of learning and culture.

5. Open plain, or meadow.

Smoke in various places of the mountains – mountains richly diversified

Stroll out of the town towards the paseo [1] and make a tour to the river

[13] visit the chapel of our lady of the fountain of health – a small image of the virgin was found in a fountain or well & had endowed its waters with miraculous salutary qualities – a chapel is now erected & various votive offerings testify the efficacy of the fountain – a burst gun is hung up & a picture showing that a man was wounded in the hand by its bursting but – calling on our lady of the fountain his wound was instantly cured – Pleasant walk between the old Moorish walls & the river – Trees tho not yet in leaf ruins of Moorish mill under the walls – large bridge over the Guadalquivir with Moorish tower at one end – We embark in small boat and are rowed about the Guadalquivir opposite to the town – New Quay partly finished of granite [14] with Marble parapets. It has been thirty years constructing, but frequently interrupted –

Streets of Cordova narrow & confused – no magnificence of architecture – all white washed which gives uniformity – & somewhat of monotony – appears to be clean – Have interior courts with orange trees

1. The Paseo de la Victoria, just outside the ancient Moorish walls of Cordova.

saw a fine palm tree in one part of the city – Houses with flowers at the balconies – windows smaller than at Madrid

Evening stroll in the cathedral its wilderness of aisles & colums in deep obscurity with here and there the light dimly gleaming before some saint or altar – a forest of pillars – The exterior gates and some of the interior chapels [15] have texts from the coran inscribed in gilt or coloured letters on the cornices

In the cathedral there is a small circular chapel beautifully adorned with Moorish painting gilding and mosaic work in christal – The Moslems used to walk with bare feet round its walls repeating their prayers and there are chanls worn in the pavement.

In another part of the cathedral a pillar is shewn with a feeble[?] representation of our saviour on the cross scratched on it – which it is said was done by a christian prisoner with his nails – when chained to the pillar to worship in the Mahometan manner

[16] At our Inn – great paved hall below – filled with muleteers – with packs of merchandize about to depart for a complete caravan – courtyard likewise full – fine grapes – some eating & drinking – others sleeping others loading their mules –

In the evening while we sup guns are brought in &

stood in a corner – Muleteers – or peasants just arrived – one looks in and has the air more of a robber
than a peasant – Wild roving hardy life of these
people – every man mounts his mule with his pack
of merchandize – his alforjas [1] before him & his gun
slung behind his saddle [17] his andaluzian hat –
short jacket – sash & belt, breeches with a hundred
buttons & his embroiderd leathern gaiters & his
never failing brown mantle These people preserve
the arab look & arab manner & to see them at a
distance coming over these great naked plains one
might suppose himself transported to Africa

[18] *March 5* Wednesday – get up early & see the sun
rise – lighting up the bridge the old Moorish tower
& mill & the course of the Guadalquivir – The sun
the great alchemist of nature.

The Canon Don   [2] Trevilla nephew of the Bishop
calls on us, a small man with one eye about 32 –
accompanys us over the cathedral shews us the Episcopal library – Librarian shewing rare copies of bible
– says the[y] are seldom read – that the people here
are dolts – The canon accompanies us in an excur-
sion up the mountain of Sierra Morena to the Hermitage [3] – the Superior shews us about the place.

1. Saddlebags.
2. Irving's blank.
3. Las Ermitas, in the Sierra de Córdoba, four miles north of
Cordova, known as the "desierto de Belén."

Each hermit has his little mansion – his garden &
commands a [19] delicious view over a great front
of Andalusia – The rich valley of the Guadalquivir
– Andujar at one end – Almodovar on its promontory at the other – the mountains of Jaen the pike
of Martos [1] – the Sierra Nevada of Granada – the
Alpuxarras [2] – country like a historic map – full of
history & romance where the Moors & christians
have fought – Scenes of scamper[?] and enterprize
& foray – Sides of the mountain covered with flowers
& odoriferous shrubs – but I missed the song of the
bird & the hum of the bee & not a single butterfly
had yet sallied forth upon his spring campaign – The
trees have scarce yet put forth their tender [20] leaves
yet the bosom of the earth is soft & fresh & reeking
with odours – The air is suave – We see around us
the aloes – the fig trees, the vine and many other
plants of the South

   We had our horses led to the foot of the mountain
& walked down
After dinner we walked out with the canon – and a
younger canon and Doctor – and an old colonel to

1. The Peña de Martos (Peak of Martos), near the town of Martos, in the southwestern part of the province of Jaén. From this,
by the order of Ferdinand IV in 1312, were hurled the Carvajal
brothers.
2. This mountainous district of the Alpujarras in Andalusia includes
the two provinces of Granada and Almería.

the Alameda [1] of the Bishop – a countryseat on the banks of the Guadalquivir with walks of oranges – citrons – myrtle &c and a fountain in the center of a small garden. In the heats of summer they must be delicious – The trees hang into the waters of the Guadalquivir – returned [21] home between hedges of aloes & Indian Fig – The Almond trees just ready to put forth their blossoms Old Moorish Alcazar [2] – Since the Inquisition – now the prison – gate way of yellow stone opposite the Bridge

Thursday 6 March. In the morning make arrangements for Horses to take us to Granada 4 hours for 45$. The muleteer & horses found – visit the Archiepiscopal palace [3] – very simple – House of the Conde – afternoon ride up to convent of St Jeronimo [4] –

1. Irving probably refers to the "Alameda del Corregidor" (Grove of the Mayor), which is a short distance below the bridge over the Guadalquivir, just outside the town.
2. This royal palace, built by the Arabs during the reign of Abderrahmán in the latter half of the eighth century, was used successively by the Convent of San Agustín (1312–1328), by the Governor of the Province, and by the Inquisition. Since 1821 it has been employed as a public jail or prison.
3. The Palacio Episcopal. The older part of this palace was built in the fifteenth century; the newer portions were constructed by Bishop Leopold of Austria.
4. This old convent, probably built of stone from the ruins of the famous summer palace of the Moors, Medina Azzahara, is about five miles from Cordova, on the Serranía de Córdoba. Irving described this convent fully in letters. *E.g.*: "While at Cordova we made excursions on horseback among the heights of the Sierra

fine view – visit the Albayda ¹ an old moorish house
in castle – an old mill [22] there – beautiful ride
along the skirts of the Sierra Morena Our two
guides – the driver of the Horse & his brother In
the evening hear stories of 11 robbers mounted – on
the Rambla road ² – engage an escort of 4 men meet
the Canon & take leave – The old Col Francisco
Oviedo calls on us & gives letters to person in Castro ³
[23] Friday 7. rise at 4 o'clock. pack. – Horses
arrive – when about to start Dilligence arrives. Mʳ
Shaw & two fellow travellers – one an American –
the other an Englishman clergyman Mr Tomlinson
The Am. & Eng. propose to join us – Have to find
five more horses – additional escort – one who guards

Morena which rise behind the city, visiting the celebrated hermitage
and the convent of St. Geronimo. The mountains were clothed with
aromatic shrubs, and with flowers which in other countries are the
forced productions of gardens and hothouses. From these heights
the eye revels over a delicious landscape; a broad green valley
fertilized by the windings of the shining Guadalquivir, and bounded
by long lines of mountains famous in the hardy predatory wars of
the Moors and Christians. The snowy summit of the Sierra Nevada
lies like a brilliant cloud in the distance, marking the situation of
Granada, the city of romantic history." Irving to Mademoiselle
Antoinette Bolviller, Granada, March 15, 1828, P.M.I., II, 287.

1. A summer place built by the caliphs of Cordova, a mile or two
outside the city.

2. The road leading to the town of La Rambla.

3. Castro del Río, a town of about twelve thousand inhabitants,
southeast of Cordova.

the diligence & has been a robber – Bustle at Inn –
Men in capas [1] – looking suspicious Mr Gessler loses
his purse.

Set off at 8 oclock – fine view of Cordova from the
heights – road passes over lonely naked hills – partly
cultivated with grain – rarely a hovel of shepherd.
here and there a flock of sheep or goats – pass crosses
at three places where [24] travellers have been murdered – Our companions have an escort who has
been a robber – stout man with fierce eye – at $\frac{1}{2}$
past 12 stop at a steep ford – a cortijo [2] where there
are several huts – dine under a shed from the con-
tents of our wallet – resume our march – pass along
an agreeable little valley watered by a small river
which we ford – about 4 oclock arrive at Castro del
rio [3] – Situated in the same little valley – nearly cir-
cled by the winding river – neighboring hills bare,
but at present green old walls with square & round
towers – large Moorish tower – Houses of the town
whitewashed – patios in the center – call on Don
Benito Paulo vicario de [25] Castro – with letter
from Don Francisco Oviedo – get order from Commandant for 4 escorts – They demand 16 Dollars to
go to Granada & return – offer them 12 –

1. Capes, or cloaks.
2. A farmhouse, and the land surrounding it.
3. See p. 13, footnote 3.

Two captains of the escorts who turn out to be rogues – play a double game between us & Don Benito – The latter calls on us & their tricks are discov^d – Commandant sends us 4 Grenadiers – picked men who are to go for 12$.

Supper – Gessler makes omlet – Gessler, Stoffregen & I sleep in one room on two thin mattresses spread on the floor – wrapped in our cloaks – In the night toward morning serenade of friars with lanterns [26] on poles singing pecado mortal [1] –

8. Saturday – preparations for departure – uproar at Inn Regidor of Priego [2] with his companion & servant man in a fury with the Landlady – he had lost his cloak & gun – It is discovered that one of our escorts of yesterday had stole them. He is caught & cuffed kicked & punished by all hands & carried off to prison – We set out at $\frac{1}{2}$ past 6 – Overtaken by Regidor of Priego – & his companions – Active wiry man – iron gray hair – two muskets slung behind his saddle – his servant the same – Dreary ride through hilly country – Green little valley with small river run- [27]ning through it – little river of Sjuan[?] [3] –

1. "Mortal sin," probably words from the friars' chant.
2. Alderman or magistrate of Priego de Córdoba, a town of about seventeen thousand inhabitants in the southeastern part of the province of Cordova.
3. This word is illegible. Perhaps the river San Juan.

About midday pass Baena [1] – Sun burnt town on hill – castle large olive hills around – little brook in valley below – Great picturesque mountains to the South east – Stop at a fountain near it – take lunch – & let the horses drink – picturesque scene of soldiers – horses – guides &c –

toilsome ascent of mountains – solitary watch towers – Stop for a short time at La Rabita [2] – Sunset – Look over Mountains – After sunset arrive at the Summit of the Mountain – see the snowy heights of Sierra Nevada – get benighted – lose our way – wander across ploughed grounds [28] keeping the castle of Alcala la Real [3] in sight – arrive there at $\frac{1}{2}$ past 7 – Supper – eggs – Ham which we brought with us – Sleep in two alcoves – three in one two in other – Landlady who speaks in whispers – two pretty daughters –

9 – Morning – Alcala in gorge of Mountain tops – Castle on one summit – with street leading down to fountain & church. Hermitage or chapel on the other

1. A town of some fifteen thousand people, southeast of Cordova and Castro del Río.
2. A village in the province of Jaén between Baena and Alcalá la Real.
3. A township of about fifteen thousand inhabitants in the province of Jaén. The town itself, with a population of about six thousand and situated near the foot of the Monte de la Cruces and the Monte de la Mota, is of Moorish origin, and was the scene of many struggles between Arab and Spaniard.

[30] [1] Stop at a venta [2] at Puerto Lope [3] – house bears marks of balls – Atalayas [4] on the hills – little green valley – Snowy mountains peeping over it – Eagles soaring – Repast on rude table in the venta – Deep chimney in one corner in which are seated the soldiers & family – We are surrounded by Dogs and fowls – Leaving this place we continue on winding down the mountains until we come in sight of the vega of Granada – Stop at Pinos de la puente [5] – Small village – narrow bridge over a small but rapid stream – defile at foot of mountain of Elvira – we wind round [31] the foot of this Stern mountain & at length come in sight of the city of Granada – Stop at a venta in the Vega – where are a number of ruffian looking peasants – one wants us to drink wine with him – Continue on – one long lank fellow accompanys our escort – in a kind of uniform – a hen tied by the legs & slung over his shoulder on the end of his sabre – Approach to Granada between hedges & olive orchards & vineyards – Vegetation

1. On p. [29] Irving drew a sketch of mountains with the inscription "Puerto of —— with two atalayas or watch towers in advance." Of seven other words only two are legible: "puerto" and "shining."
2. An inn.
3. Puerto López, a small village.
4. Watch towers.
5. Pinos-Puente, with a population of about forty-five hundred persons, at the foot of the Sierra Elvira, about six miles northwest of the city of Granada.

not yet out – Most of the trees merely in bud & the smallest leaf – Sun sets just as we enter Granada [1] – beautiful appearance of the city – Have difficulty in finding lodgings – the Fonda de la paz being shut up at length put up at Fonda [2]

[32] Name of our Robber guide Bautista Serrano de Ecija [3]

[33] *March 10.* Call on Banker Sen[r] Pedro Dandega[?] & get 50 $ on the letter of credit of M[r] Roberts. [4] – Visit the Alhambra with Mr Gessler – find there M[r] Tomlinson – Mr. Wilson – joined by M[r] Stoffregen – After visiting the various apartments of the Alhambra we return to dinner – and after dinner – about 4 oclock ascend to the garden of the Generalife & above that to the Silla del Moro [5] from whence we see a superb sunset – behind the Mountains of Loxa [6] – The convent bells ringing the Angelus

[34] *March 11.* Call on the Governor of Granada Don [7] in company with M[r] Gessler & M[r] Stoffregen.

1. See P.M.I., II, 287; S.T.W., I, 329.
2. Irving omitted the name of this fonda.
3. See P.M.I., II, 284.
4. Possibly David Roberts, the painter. See S.T.W., II, 317.
5. The Silla del Moro (Chair of the Moor) commands a superb view of the Alhambra and of the Sierra Nevada.
6. Loja, west of Granada, a town with about nineteen thousand inhabitants.
7. Irving's blank.

Afterwards visit the Archbishop Don   [1] Palma.
Find him at dinner – with canon &c – Experience
very kind reception. Invites me to dine every day
at the Palace which I decline. Engage to go the day
after tomorrow to see his palace in the country.

After dinner take a walk along the promenade constructed on the banks of the Xenil [2] – See the chapel
of S Sebastians, formerly a mosque – The place
where Chiquito [3] took leave of Fernando & Isabella.

[35] *March 12*. Wednesday. Visit the arch Bishop
with M[r] Stoffregen & M[r] Gessler – return home &
write letters – Send letters today to Peter – & to M[r]
& Susan Storrow [4] – after dinner walk to Alhambra
with comp[ns] de voyage & Sen[r]   [5] See the interior
of Palace of Ch[s.] V. In the Alhambra, find the governor of it with several priests & ladies – See the
interior of the chapel – anciently mosque –

1. Irving's blank.
2. The Genil River which flows by the city on the south, and crosses
the Vega. The "promenade" is probably the present Paseo de la
Bomba.
3. Boabdil el Chico, the Moorish king, who on January 2, 1492
surrendered the keys of Granada to King Ferdinand, at the chapel of
San Sebastián. See pp. 21, 71. See also *The Alhambra, passim*.
4. Thomas Wentworth Storrow, an English business man living in
Paris with his family (among them his daughter, Susan Storrow),
was an intimate friend of Irving's. See *Washington Irving and the
Storrows. Letters from England and the Continent 1821–1828*, ed. S. T.
Williams, Cambridge, Massachusetts, 1933. Probably the letter
dated March 10, 1828. See *idem*, pp. 127–129.
5. Irving's blank.

[36] March 13 *Thursday* – at ½ past 6 Mʳ Tomlinson & Mʳ Wilson set off on horseback for Malaga – At nine oclock – Mʳ Stoffregen, Mʳ Gessler & myself set off on horseback to visit the Archbishops palace at Besna[?] [1] – ride up the mountain – Olive trees – country houses about the hills – Besna a small hamlet depending upon the Palace – Find at the Palace the Major Domo – & his step son a handsome boy of 13 or 14 Page to the archbishop – palace filled with bad & old paintings Patio painted with exploits of Don Quixote – myrtle & orange trees – fountains playing – take wine & Sausages – ride up to [37] source of a flow of water which supplies the Albaicin – large basin of chrystal water – boiling up in various places – Trees on the bank –

Return to Archbishops country seat – dine in Hall – sound of fountain – walk in garden commandg view over the vega – return to Granada – beautiful view as we approach foot of mountain – Evg at Theater – concert – Madre Morales daughter of Garcia [2] sings

[38] Friday March 14. Visit the Cathedral – Tomb

1. This word is almost illegible. Perhaps Béznar, a village of about eight hundred inhabitants, southeast of Granada.
2. Probably the singer and composer Manuel García (1775–1832), famous both on the Continent and in America. In 1825 he brought his operatic company to the United States. With him was his daughter María, generally known as "La Malibrán."

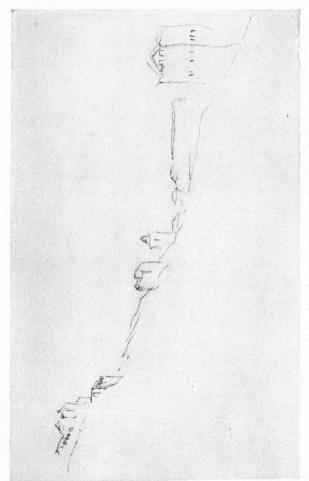

Irving's Sketch of a Portion of the Alhambra

of Ferdinand & Isabella – with Princes – Paintings
of Murillo &c – ascend the tower – old man & woman
who live in the tower – From the summit there is a
panoramic view of the city & environs –
visit the Archbishop –
visit convent of St Domingo – garden & Pavillion
formerly retreat of Moorish Kings – immense Lau-
rels which form coverd walks – Baths.
Figures of Ferdinand & Isabella in the church
After dinner walk up the valley of the Darro. Deep
ravine with small brook winding thro it. orchards.
vineyards &c road cut along Pass of the hills –
[42] [1] *Saturday 15*. Visit Monte Santo with Gessler –
Stoffregen & brother of Duke of   [2]

subterranean place where Saint[s] were burnt –
& where lead books were found –

Ride round the Alhambra – meet with Mateo
Ximenes [3] – leave my companions and accompy
Mateo in search of the gate by which Chiquito
sallied.[4]

1. On pp. [39, 40, 41] Irving drew sketches of the Alhambra and of
the surrounding country.
2. Irving's blank.
3. Irving's most important friendship in Granada, both now and
during his second visit in 1829, was with this Spanish peasant, Mateo
Ximénez, who acted as his guide and who told him many tales
which later appeared in Irving's book (*The Alhambra*, 1832). See
S.T.W., Chap. XV, *passim*.
4. See *The Alhambra*, London, 1832, I, 169.

Write letters to Mll Bolviller [1] – Mr Antoine[?] Dou-
bril [2] – Mr Arndt

[43] Gate by which Chiquito sallied – The tower
is rent & great masses lie around half coverd with
huge vines & spreading fig trees – almond trees in
blossom – butterflies [3]

Cross glen to convent of the Martyrs

[44] Sunday 16 – Visit Cathedral – & church of S^t
Jeronimo – walk up the valley of the Darro to the
fountain of   [4] climb to the Silla del Moro view
from Silla dcl Moro at 1 oclock – to the right the valley of Darro – beyond the Albaycin – below me the
Generaliffe with its cypress trees beyond the Alhambra – beyond the city & vega – To the right Zubia [5]
– before us Alhendin [6] – Mount of Loja in distance
– pigeons flying about generaliffe [45] voices from

1. Mlle. Antoinette Bolviller, a niece of M. D'Oubril, the Russian
minister at Madrid. Irving wrote her many delightful letters. See
P.M.I., II, 285–292, 297–304, etc. Of these two letters the former is
that mentioned in this Journal, on March 15, 1828. See also S.T.W.,
Index.
2. M. D'Oubril, the French minister at Madrid, with whose family
Irving was intimate. See S.T.W., Index.
3. At this point in the Journal Irving drew a sketch of a part of the
Alhambra, with the caption: "command[s] view of vega – Darro &c
vega with Darro."
4. Irving's blank.
5. A town of about thirty-five hundred people, three miles southeast
of Granada, in the foothills of the Sierra Nevada.
6. A village of some two thousand inhabitants, about five miles
south of Granada.

the valley of the Darro – Birds singing – bees hum-
ming by me – vega in blossom & young leaf – gleams
of the Xenil – Distant murmur of the city like the sea
– cocks crowing – Opposite side of Darro – mountain
full of holes retreats of gipsies – Indian Fig – aloes –
horses & mules passing along opposite side –

In Vega see Hermitage of St Sebastian [1] where
Chiquito surrendered [2]

[47] [3] Monday March 17. Sunrise seated on the
Monte de los Martyros [4] – The Alhambra to my
right – The Vega before me – Bells sounding from
the city – part of which spreads from the skirt of the
mountain beneath my feet – Alhambra reddening in
the sun shine – sound of running water – cocks crowing – smoke rising from various parts of city – towns
& villages in the vega more visible than in evening –
See Zubia Alenden Amilla [5] &c &c &c – Vega every
day more tinted with blossoms –

Sound of voices of gipsies the vermin which infest
these heights – Convent bell of Los Martiros – Sun
begins to gleam along the vega and light up spires
& houses

1. See p. 75.
2. See *The Alhambra*, London, 1832, I, 171.
3. P. [46] Irving left blank.
4. The Campo de los Mártires, which is part of the hill called
Alhambra.
5. Irving refers to Alhendín, and to Armilla, a small village about
two miles from Granada.

[48] Alhambra guarded by old men who can hardly shoulder their muskets 9 cypress trees in the entrance of the torre de la Vela [1] –

Torres Vermejas [2] on a separate height
In the prospect of the Vega there are high snowy mountains beyond Alhendin

Morning about sun rise – Monk in white mantle – with black under it & broad white hat sallying forth on cruise

effect of early sunshine along the green woods bottom of Alhambra sparkling among the young leaves – [51] [3] Hailed by Mateo Ximenes from the walls of the Alhambra – later & walk with him among the towers. Visit the Tower of Las Infantas. [4] Lofty chamber within, with balconies &c. where the Moorish female was seen

1. Famous since the day of the capture of the Alhambra (January 12, 1492), when the cross of Cardinal Mendoza, the standard of the Apostle Santiago (St. James), and the banners of King Ferdinand were placed upon this tower.

2. The three towers (Torres Bermejas) forming a large fortress, which was partly rebuilt in the sixteenth century.

3. On p. [49] Irving drew a sketch of the country visible from los Mártires. The places named include Mártires, Zubia, Gabia, Alhendín, Armilla. Four names are illegible. On p. [50] he drew a sketch of mountains with the caption: "Snowy summits of Sierra Montibibi[?]." He names Gabia la Chica, Gabia el grande, and Churriana. Two other names are illegible.

4. The Torre de los Infantes, built at the end of the fourteenth century, is a perfect model of a small Arab dwelling. See *The Alhambra*, London, 1832, I, 279–282.

Visit his old Fathers house and garden. The house half painted – built of reeds & plaister – The old man builds it himself. They are Ribband weavers – buy 4 pieces of ribband of them for 4$ pays 28 rials a year rent for garden.[1]

return home about 9 – Breakfast & then ride out with Stoffregen & Gessler & brother of the Duke of Gor [2] to the convent of St Iago on the road to Guadix. Road winds up among the mountains. Convent vast & dreary – The severe order of   [3] The monks never enter cities – The superior of the convent & order attended us – a stout, pleasant man. Cano [4] was for two years a kind of prisoner in this convent and filled it with his paintings. The French have carried off many. The English have purchased some – There are [52] several fine ones left. The Trinity over the altar piece – paintings of Saints each side of it. A Virgin & child – a side altar on the right – A St Iago to left of grand altar. An Assumption on the stair case &c

1. Irving's references to money are puzzling. He uses the dollar sign as indicated, but the price he here names for ribbons is almost as absurd as the annual rent for the garden, which at the present value of the real (about three cents) would amount to about eighty-five cents.
2. A close friend who made his library available to Irving, and who sought him out years later when Irving was minister to Spain, in 1842. See S.T.W., I, 367–368; II, 142–143.
3. Irving's blank.
4. Probably Alonso Cano (1601–1667), famous Spanish painter, sculptor, and architect.

There are four fine paintings of St Augustine –
S^t [1] in the choir – The Superior said he was
absent when the French took the paintings – Had he
been at the convent they should not have had them.
He would have been hanged first.

Return to town & then sally forth on horseback
with guide and ride to valley of Zubia. Pass thro the
vega – by two houses formerly belonging to the
Moors – one at present a farm house: the other a
chapel. Zubia on the skirts of a Hill. On entering
past the convent of St Francisco on the left founded
by Ferdinand & Isabella in commemoration of the
battle.[2] Laurel in the garden of the [53] Convent,
said to have shaded the Queen. Turn the first street
to the right: enter the house of a Labrador [3] – Francisco Garcia House formerly royal – royal arms
painted on ceilings – Proprietor shows us all over it.
It is said that the Queen contemplated the battle
from the Summit of this house – The owner said he
had that morning been reading romance of Gar-

1. Irving's blank.
2. While looking down on Granada, on August 25, 1491, during the
siege, Queen Isabella and her guard were suddenly surrounded by a
large force of Arabs. During the ensuing struggle, the Queen, praying
in a grove of laurel, vowed, if her warriors were successful, to found
here a monastery dedicated to St. Louis (whose saint's day it was).
Such was the origin of the ancient convent of San Luis de la Zubia,
or San Luis el Real, which was torn down in 1843.
3. Farmer or country squire.

cilasso de la Vega[1] – When we ret[d] down stairs
I asked after it He brought it to me – I wanted
to keep it & offered money to the children – He pre-
sented me with it but would receive no money in
exchange – His wife talked of the novel translated
from the French of Gonzalo of Cordova.[2] They in-
vited me to eat something – I found afterwards from
my guide that this woman had been of good parent-
age of Granada reduced[?]

On leaving Zubia pass ruins of a Moorish tower –
Beautiful view of Granada on the way back along
skirts of hills –

[54][3] After dinner visit the painter of the Theater –
Afterward walk along the Xenil – Visit M[r] Firado[?]
– afterward the Count de Teba[4] – a most agreeable
man. Sadly cut up in the wars – lost one eye –
maimed of a leg – a hand wounded by bursting of a
gun. Talks of the earthquakes of Granada.

Generalife in possession of count of   [5] descendant of Chiquito

1. Garcilaso de la Vega (1503–1536), famous Spanish poet. "Romance" is used in the Spanish sense of short poem or ballad.
2. Gonzalo Fernández de Córdoba (1453–1515), distinguished Spanish general, known as the "Gran Capitán." He was the hero of the
novel mentioned by Irving.
3. At the bottom of this page [54], upside down, Irving wrote the
following words: "Avilleneda Cronic[a] del Rey Don Pedro."
4. See The Alhambra, London, 1829, II, 6 ff.
5. Irving's blank.

Garcilasso de la Vega [1] who killed Tarfe afterwards distinguished himself in America

[55] *Tuesday 18.* Set out on promenade on horseback
with Mr Gessler – Horses bad – dismount & go up
to Alhambra –

Visit the Tower of Infantas – Old hall inside –
Smoky walls – Solitary tortoise shell cat – bird cage
hanging up – Be quiet – the haunts of the princess
– balconies

Fig trees & almond trees about the tower

Governor of Alhambra Don Francisco de Cerna

[56] In the Generalife – Picture of Ponce de Leon
– of middle size – hair & beard short & black – ruff
round his neck which renders the picture apocryphal
– steel & gilt armour truncheon – dagger & sword
– helm with white plumes – trunk hose white stock-
ings & white shoes

Garcilasso de la vega – Helm without feathers – steel
from head to foot – truncheon

Rey Chico [2] – mild handsome face – fair – yellow

1. Hernán Pérez del Pulgar entered Granada by the conduit of
the Darro on the night of December 18, 1490, and with his dagger
pinned to the door of the mosque a scroll bearing the words "Ave
María." He regained the Christian camp in safety. The Moor
Zegrí Tarfe, bringing back the scroll to the Christians, defied them
to single combat, and was slain by Garcilaso de la Vega.
2. This picture of Boabdil, like every incident connected with the
unfortunate king, made a profound impression upon Irving. See
S.T.W., I, 347.

hair blk crown with gold on top yellow brocade
dress – Blk velvet over it

[57] Hernando de Pulgar [1] – Delicate and elderly
man short gray hair moustaches & beard – gray eyes
– ruff trunk hose – white tight leather boots

Genealogical tree of the family of Don Pedro de
Granada Venegas Caballero del Abito de St Iago
& Senores de Campotexar Iayena[?] &c – made
to descend from Teodofredo Principe Godo & –
called by the Moors Abdala – & heir of Moorish
kings of Saragossa & Granada.[2]

[58] Picture of Dona Juana de Mendoza – Lady of
honor of Queen Isabella & wife of Don Alonzo de
Granada Venegas

senora [3] de Campotexa[r] fair complexion – yellow

1. See *idem*, I, 367–368.
2. This is an extremely difficult and almost illegible passage. Campotéjar is a small village in the province of Granada, and for several
centuries the owners of the Generalife were the marqueses of
Campotéjar. The Order of Santiago is a Spanish military order
founded in the kingdom of León in 1161, to protect the country from
invasions. The Order became very powerful, and played an important part in the wars with the Moors. After the time of Ferdinand
and Isabella the title of "Caballero de Santiago" became merely
honorary. "Caballero del Hábito de Santiago" means "Knight of
the Military Order of St. James." Fragmentary as this entry in the
Journal is, it is an interesting example of Irving's antiquarianism in
preparation for his *The Conquest of Granada* (1829) and *The Alhambra*
(1832). See *The Conquest of Granada*, pp. 85–86.
3. Preceding this word in the manuscript are two marks which re-
semble the numeral 11. This is probably a slip of Irving's pen.

hair pearl coloured brocade dress Dark velvet mantle trimmed with fur & clasped with pearls. Ornaments of head necklace – ears [1] &c of pearl

On our return from Generaliffe we pass by the Torres Vermejas [2] – supposed by some to be built by the Phenecians by others by the Romans – They are certainly older than the Alhambra – Stop at the man who makes figures in clay – beautiful view from his little terraced [59] garden. Take leave of the archbishop

After dinner Count Teba calls for us & takes us in his carriage to the convent of Carthusians [3] – Severe order – eat no meat – Do not converse with each other except on certain occasions – Splendid chapel – beautiful particol[d] marbles – dark greenish marble – chapel gay and stuccoed in bad taste – Inlaid commodes of tortoiseshell &c – made by a monk – fishpond with terrapins for the convent table – Prior a pleasant man – burly & laughing – took us to see the cell of one of the brothers – dormitory – little sitting room – small garden &c –

Afterward we take a promenade with Count Teba into the vega along the canal – rich & beautiful scenery – groves of cherries, almonds, nuts – mulberries, Figs, oranges – vines &c

1. Earrings.   2. See p. 24, footnote 2.
3. La Cartuja, a monastery founded early in the sixteenth century.

[60] passed Evg at Count De Tebas – says the origin
of Story of Don Juan is in Hist of Pedro the Cruel
Mss.[1] The Statue of the Commandant is in the
Chapel of the Family of Ulloa –

After leaving the count we go to Mr Almeya – and
arrange about horses – Family scene – The old pa-
triarch – his cousins – his daughter & her lover a
young man of Malaga the young people had been
performing on pianoforte

[61] Wednesday 1 P[M] Day of St Jose[2] Capilla Real –
grand altar – wooden relief of Surrender of Granada
– Moor sallying forth – His white horse led after him
– King Queen & Grand Cardinal – latter on mule –
Baptism of Moors of Campotexar[?] –

Tombs of Ferd & Isabella & of Philip le Bell &
Juana la folle [3]

[62] Wednesday afternoon ½ past 4 – In the mirador [4]
of the Queens tower Sun shine resting gloriously upon
the towers of the Alhambra and the Sierra Nevada –
Mixture of trees & town – Sound of water Generalife
in full sunshine – In summer the trees are full of

1. Irving almost certainly refers to *Crónicas del rey don Pedro*, written by Pero López de Ayala (1332–1402), the eminent historian and
poet of the fourteenth century.
2. March 19 is the Day of St. Joseph.
3. The Infanta Joanna ("Juana la Loca"), daughter of Ferdinand
and Isabella, who named Philip of Austria, King Philip I of
Spain.
4. Belvidere, oriel, bay window.

nightingales – which sing continually – especially in moonlight nights

Hermitage of S[t] Michael [1] – on Summit of hill above Albaycin

[63] ½ past 6 – from the top of the tower of Las Infantas – delicious view over the Alhambra – Granada the Vega – hazy distance with the sun blazing thro it – gleams of water in vega – green Sheets of plain – Song from the side of the Hill de los martyros [2] – guitar – party on the hill females dancing – Sound of water from the ravine below the tower –

Goats feeding about the Alhambra –

Interior of tower – Smoky – fountain paved up – formerly the water sucked into it – tortoise shell cat – Kitchen in the 2[d] Story

[64] Torre of Los Captivos [3] – Ivy – peach & Plum trees apricots – water running thro the glen – walls of glen over hung with grapes – figs – Ivy – myrtle – Jessamine – Old battlements of curtains [4] which connect towers – Sunshine on towers

1. The Ermita de San Miguel, occupying the site of an old Arab fort called Torre del Aceituno, which in 1753 was replaced by a shrine. This was destroyed by the French in 1812, and rebuilt in 1828.
2. See p. 23.
3. The Torre de la Cautiva, built by Yûsuf I, and restored in 1873–1876. Its name is derived from the erroneous belief that Isabel de Solís was imprisoned here.
4. The part of a bastioned front connecting two neighboring bastions.

[65] 6 P[M] – Garden of the Generalife Sun going down – over the tower of the Vela – between the town & the cypress trees – bells ringing – guns firing salvo echoes of mountains – birds singing – people on distant hills dancing Suavity of air – birds singing – beauty of Vega – down from Alhambra – Cypress trees of the Generalife – Silver crescent of the Moon –

[66] Galery above in the Generalif portraits of Fernando & Isabella – good. Philip Bel & Juana la folle – Hernando Pulgar Grand Capitan – excellent Alonzo De Aguilar [1] – Noble rather bald – Truncheon in rest – Noble calm air

[67] Don Jose Ochoa who slew the 4 Moors
March 20 – Leave Granada [2] at 9 oclock with horses of   [3] Garcia – rich scene leaving the city by the bridge near Hermitage [4] – horses drink of fountain – Roads full of people – rich belt of orchards.

pass thro neat village of Armilla – Alhendin [5] on a rising ground surrounded by olives – & peaceful fields at   [6]

1. Alonso de Aguilar was one of the conquistadores who came to America with Quesada, and settled in Colombia. See also p. 69.
2. See S.T.W., I, 330.
3. Irving's blank.
4. Probably the Ermita de San Sebastián.
5. See p. 23, footnote 5.
6. Irving's blank.

[69] [1] At 11 oclock Suspiro of Moor [2] – Dry Hills – cross opposite the stone on which the Moor stood – Mules coming up the path – Lark singing

[72] [3] Padul [4] – at the foot of Mounts in a little vega or green basin high and mounts one with Snow – Slate – beds of mount^n torrents – filled with shingle – olive orchards – our squadron of horse & mule – escopetas [5] &c little castle at Padul – Cross on top of hill before coming to it – murderd traveller

Valley formerly a lake – deep pit of   [6] fathoms[?]

[73] *Berja* [7] – Zubia – valley among olive trees Venta on brow of hill – Shed before it man sitting in shade muleteer about going off – road winding down steep hill Muleteer going down escopetas – deep rough valley – river from snowy mount^s – mills, river of roaring water – olive trees rocks – town of Zubia

1. On p. [68] Irving drew a sketch, with the caption: "Suspiro del Moro ½ past 11 March 20." See illustration facing p. 34.
2. "El Ultimo Suspiro del Moro," the place where Boabdil turned to gaze for the last time on the city which he had lost. Of this sentimental legend Irving was extremely fond. See *The Alhambra*, London, 1832, I, 172.
3. On p. [70] Irving drew a sketch of mountains with the title "ultimo suspiro." P. [71] is blank.
4. A town of about five thousand inhabitants, some thirteen miles from Granada, on the highway between this city and Motril.
5. Guns.
6. Irving's blank.
7. A town of about six thousand inhabitants, in the province of Almería. For Zubia, see p. 34, footnote 5.

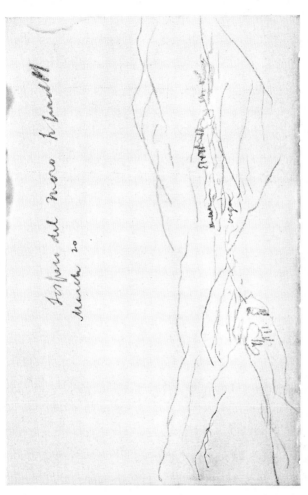

Irving's Sketch of the "Suspiro del Moro"

Berjah (Berja) situated on a very pretty river called by the Moors Wadi-adhra [1] the river of Adra whose banks are coverd with trees & flowers.

When one comes to Berja says a Moorish poet one has no alternative but to stop there for its houses & gardens are so many paradises but the roads leading to them are so many hells

Vol. I P. 53 Gayangos [2] translator of al Makhari Berja the Bergi of Pliny & Strabo [3]

[74] Lunch at Venta

Cuesta del Torrente [4] – before coming to it we see to the left Niguela [5] – ——

The deep ravines are not seen until you arrive at them

In traversing these Mountains there is a singular vicissitude of scenery At one time you are in a desert wild and mountain – Then you come into a deep rich valley – with aloes – oranges citrons myrtle vines figs &c – rocks hung with myrtle – valleys are rich

1. The word Uadi (or Wadi, in English) is a common name for rivers in Arabia and Africa, and is also applied to river valleys.
2. Pascual Gayangos y Arce (1809–1897), historian and scholar. He later became Irving's personal friend. See S.T.W., Index.
3. Pliny mentions an island of this name, which has been said to be Bergen, Norway. In ancient times there was also a town called Bergi, in Hispania, which some believe to be the modern Almería.
4. Hill of the Torrent.
5. Nigüelas, a village of about one thousand inhabitants, in the province of Granada, on the southern slope of the Sierra Nevada, in the valley of Lecrín. The Torrente River flows by this village.

shalows on banks of mountains – goats [75] Muleteers winding down rocks & precipices – Deep beds
of Torrents dry or with silver threads of water winding thro them but which in their fury have tumbled
huge rocks

Pass the Bridge of Tableta[?]

Connecting two sides of a deep ravine – Jagged with
rocks like teeth – Saldiva the Guerilla who fighting
with the french fell with his horse down the precipice
& was not killed

– Pass man returning from laboring in the vineyards
[76] come singing down the Mountain

At Sunset come in sight of Lanjaron [1] – Situated
on a slope of Green – with Steep rocks below – Old
reddish yellow Moorish castle Mountains of various
cold marble – some tinged with Iron – Hung with figs,
vines – oranges – aloes – Amongst the aromatic smells
we have the sweet smell of the modest bean field

[77] In the course of the afternoon ride we pass a
hermit in brown coarse dress. Cord – rosary – long
gray beard – mounted on a Donkey – our Command [2]
salutes him graciously but afterwards tells us he is
called chief of robbers – That he tells the robbers
when any travellers are on the road & when they

1. Lanjarón, a town of some four thousand people, in the province
of Granada, on the southern slopes of the Sierra Nevada in the
valley of Lecrín. It is famous for its salt baths.
2. Irving probably means *comandante*, leader.

are likely to be – The command says that his long
gray beard seems hypocrisy.

Lanjaron Mineral baths –

[78] 21. Little square in front of the rise at Lan-
jaron – fountain – Behind it a view down a deep glen
– Trees in blossom – cliffs of various coloured stone
– Distant mountains gray.

In the square – Groups of peasants – men of the
village in cloaks – women filling vessels with water
at the fountain – fowls – Dogs – Donkies – Mules
changed – led through the place

$\frac{1}{2}$ past 8. Seated by the road side beyond Lanjaron –
in the Alpuxarras – after leaving Lanjaron we wind
up a very steep road – winding round a mountain –
view of Lanjaron [79] its flat roofed houses – ruined
castle on a broken cliff – Deep ravine with mill below & waterfall gushing from under its arches –
Lanjaron surrounded by olives oranges – Figs – vines
– Mounts clustered with chestnuts – chapel situated
on brow of hill after leaving Lanjaron

– Muleteers winding along the side of mountains –
Pass families of Gipsies – with one Donkey – Grandfather – children – grandchildren –

Seated by side of road – Sun warm – warm haze
over the mountains – Lark singing

From above Lanjaron there is a peep of the sea but
when [80] we passed it it was coverd with haze

Orgiva [1] – deep valley – green – A stream glistening thro it Church with two towers – wide ravine bed of river – aloes – figs in leaf – villages with spires high on bluffs of the Mountains

[81] After leaving Orgiva we overtake in the deep valley on bed of river a Galliard andaluz [2] mounted on a small active mule of 5 yrs old – Galliard is middlesized meagre sinewy – has brown jacket in andaluz fashion a blue trousers with hand silver lace two muskets slung behind his saddle – with the alforjas [3] – a sabre by his side – pistols – a cartridge box of crimson velvet slung over his right shoulder passing under his left arm – believe he is guard to road to protect the comings to & from the mine – we fall in company with [82] him – pass together the Puerto of Juvileo – road built up along the edge of precipices We have to walk the greater part of the way – Galliard gives us oranges out of his alforjas – Stern mountain pass —— —— [4] We cross this and pass along the bed of a river & at midday stop to dine at a venta * built on a neck of land that seems to divide two valleys formed by river which at full season must form little lakes on both sides

1. Orjiva, a town of about four thousand inhabitants in the southern part of the province of Granada, on the Guadalfeo or Cadiar River.
2. A gay Andalusian.   3. Saddlebags.
4. Two or three words are rubbed or blotted out.
* Venta of Torbiscon. [Irving's note.]

[83] Turn off from our intended route and proceed for Cadiar [1] – the village of our Galliard – who says the road is good & the place within 4 leagues of the mines – Follow up a valley with a river in the middle which at times fills the whole – the valley passes between dry mountains – arrive at Cadiar at 4 oclock – Village among olive orchards – water courses with willows – put up at miserable possada.[2] But one room for all of us – pay visit with Gall[i]ard to his cousins – His daughters had been engaged in making flowers – conversed agreeably –

[84] Don Francisco Armandrez Doña Maria Josepha Espejo en Cadiar

In the course of our ride along the river we passed a place where a venta and the little ridge on which it stood had been washed away in a night by a sudden rush of water down a valley – Only one of the inhabitants escaped by climbing to the top of the rock.

[85] 22. Leave possada at ½ past 8 Don Francisco Salido called & lent us a carbine for our protection as far as Berja – Sends a man to conduct us – Pepe the guide before starting examines his priming-lock &c – strange figures about a Spanish inn – Handsome young man wrapped in capa[3] – with fixed

1. A town of about two thousand inhabitants, in the province of Granada, on the banks of the Cadiar River.
2. *Posada:* tavern or inn.   3. Cape.

look regards us – our host a large round old man with little montera [1] – After leaving the village we pass thro narrow winding defile veritable coup-gorge [2] – our muleteer Garcia falls behind with baggage – Pepe in advance – we leave afterwards – a high hill and descend again into the bed of a river – the traverse of this mountain very threatening for' robbers – we afterwards pass along Ramblas [3] or dry beds of torrents – through wild [86] scenes of Rocks torn asunder by torrents and left dry – Sundown see Moorish looking towers – Some of the rocks seem as if torn by earthquakes – Some beautiful mount scenes = At one place we pass Between tremendous precipices of red stone overhanging the dry bed of the torrent – Caverns where fires had been made –

$\frac{1}{2}$ past 12 Stop in the dry bed of the river before the Moorish looking village of Darrica [4] and take some breakfast on a rock of marble In the course of the day we pass fig trees on which the fruit is beginning [87] to appear – Singular scene of little rich valley peeping among the wild stern rocks & moun-

1. Cloth cap.
2. *Coupe-gorge:* a dangerous spot or place.
3. Watercourses which carry off the waters of heavy rains.
4. Darrícal, a village of about a thousand inhabitants in the province of Almería, on the left bank of the Adra River. This village is about thirty-five miles from the city of Almería.

tains. Indian figs – aloes – Figs grapes pomgranites almonds –

Pass the high mountain and overlook a world of wild dry mountains – descend into the valley and arrive at Berja about 4 oclock – pass the afternoon reposing on the flat roof of our Inn. orange trees Palm – In the course of our travels thro the Alpuxarras we pass Mules laden with figs raisins Brandy &c mules with worsted bobs &c little plume of worsted – winded [?] ornaments –

Garcia singing in long drawling song about contrabandistas [1] – Ladrones [2] &c

[88] Sunday 23 – At 7 oclock we set off to ascend the Sierra De Gador to visit the mines of lead – Toilsome ascent – have often to lead the horses – view of the Mediterranean – Magnificent view over a vast extent of the Alpuxarras – Stern mountains of marble & granite, with here and there a little emerald valley locked in their iron embraces – See in a little isolated green patch the city of Orjiva the capital of the Alpuxarras – as we ascend the air grows suave fine & cool – Meet mules laden with ore – others overtake us carrying up jars of water – after four hours ascent we arrive at the mines – The whole bosom of the Mountain pierced with them – about 10,000 men in all the mines. Visit the Mine

1. Smugglers.   2. Robbers.

of Berja owned by a number of the inhabitants
[89] crawl into it – and descend creeping & crouch-
ing for some distance – & then return – miners
at their repast – Miserable looking men – feeding
out of one great dish – As we were coming off one
said farewell – we shall all meet in the Campo
Santo [1] When we came out the air was cold – Cloud
swept the summit of the Mountain with hail –
Snow in some of the pits & rifts – As we descended
it broke away and we descended into beautiful spring
and sunshine – Approach to Berja pleasant – Looks
like an oriental village – Passed thro the place re-
markably clean – with new well built houses – well
dressed people pretty women – air of prosperity after
dinner visited by our [90] Galliard Francisco Salido
who proves to be sergeant of a company of —— & de-
sirous of getting the place of his chief – Intends going
to Madrid in the summer & solicits the good word
of Stoffregen – Splendid night – brilliant moon &
stars.

[91] Monday 24 At 9 oclock set off for Adra about 2
Leagues distance – road lies along a rambla & the
bed of a small river – pleasant valley scenery – before arriving at Adra [2] we stop at a manufacture of

1. Cemetery.
2. A town of some six thousand inhabitants about nine miles from
Berja, in the province of Almería.

Lead belonging to Deputy Consul of France – arrive at Adra about ½ past 12. Small town – rebuilt on the ruins of one destroyed about 20 yrs since by an earthquake – trades in lead from the mines – deliver letter to Sr Jose   [1] nephew of M^r. Dandega – who accompanies us to Mr Kirkpatrick [2] – Windy day heavy surf

Dine with Don Jose in little room back of his shop – shoes hanging over head. Andaluz hats – his bed in a little room on one side – surrounded by goods – little Brass cows – cocks – hens – turkey cats – La petite who cooks for him – Her husband in prison in Melilla [3] – Excellent [92] dinner – fricasse of chicken – Brings out flask of Bordeaux left him by a french ship – get 32$ of him – Take tea with Mr Kirkpatrick – Hearty rough[?] old man – French consul there – The Spanish commandant –

Had to sleep 3 in a room.

[93] *Tuesday 25* – Leave Adra at 6 oclock ride along the coast – Arid mountains to our right – Blue Mediterranean to left – calm day – sea specked with sails – pass by caves – huts & cabins of fishermen – cross on a rock where traveller had been murdered –

1. Irving's blank.
2. Apparently a merchant of Málaga (Files of the United States Consulate, Málaga).
3. A Spanish possession in Morocco, directly opposite Adra on the Spanish coast.

Watch towers – pass 8 or 10 soldiers – tell them to call at inn & get ham and rice which we had left behind –

La Rabita [1] – fishing town – near a Rambla – great smuggling place in the night – small castle commanding it – with tower above it. Village partly made up of cane huts – women well dressed – some pretty – fishing boats drawn up on sand sailors playing at skittles [2] –

road winds up among hills [94] some covered with vines & figs. Stop at $\frac{1}{2}$ past 10 at Hovel on top of Hill – get fish & eggs splendid view of Mediterranean. excellent wine – family of wife & children – cottage of stones – clay – reeds &c Landlord has 8 children – possesses the surrounding land – At this place we are joined by two travellers – Spaniards – who are going beyond Motril – well mounted – with two Escopeteros [3] as guides & guards – The rest of the day a toilsome march over steep & rocky mountains – continually ascending & descending – Obliged a great part of the time to lead our horses. – Get refresh[t] of brandy & water. at hamlet of fishermen – about 4 oclock pass through [95] the village of

1. La Rábita, a small village in the township of Albuñol, in the province of Granada.
2. A game, resembling ninepins.
3. Armed men.

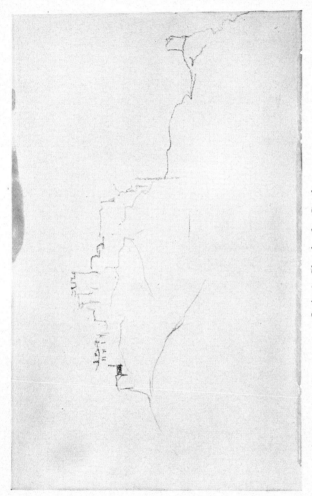

Irving's Sketch of a Castle

Guanches,[1] situated high on the breast of a mountain – commanding a noble prospect of Mediter-
ranan. Village surrounded by figs – almonds – aloes
&c – let horses drink at fountain – our fellow travellers set off ahead of us. Pepe accompanies them –
Garcia left behind. Gessler Stoffregen & myself
lose our road & wander a mile or so in wrong direction – find out our error from goatherds – Toil back
again – Horses fatigued – After passing the summit
of the Sierra we have towards sun down a splendid
view of Motril far off in a green valley – with west
mountains beyond it – purpled with the evening
haze – difft aspects of Mountains – red & [96] and
in the morning – purple & lake co^{ld} in the evening –
arrive at Motril long after sunset – by the tender
light of a half moon – pass over Rambla – among
hedges of immense figs – aloes with column 30 feet
high – Air perfumed with blossoms – put up at the
Hotel of the Catalan & have good beds & clean
rooms

In the course of the day we see a procession passing
thro the mountains in sight of ocean a dead person
coverd with linen cloth stretched on frame of cane

1. I have been unable to identify Guanches, which is what Irving
wrote. He may possibly refer to Gualchos, a village of about one
thousand inhabitants, in the extreme southern part of the province
of Granada. This village, on the slopes of a ridge called Jolúcar, is
about fifty-five miles from Granada.

placed on a mule – men & women each side of it –
[97] *Wednesday 26.* Leave Motril at 7 oclock –.
Pass along a beautiful vega – by hedges of cane &
cross a river – come to Salobrena [1] – on a rocky
height dividing a rich vega – coverd with fine vegetation – fishermen launching a boat into blue sea

[99] [2] Salobrena – rich beautiful vega each side –
running streams – Sierra nevada

– aloes – mulberrys – cotton rice – figs

fishermen launching bark – shining promontory –
boat rowing along sea –

[101] [3] Before arriving at Almunecar [4] lonely
Moorish watch tower – Hawk whirling round it –
below tower to guard ags[t] contrabandistas – pass
thro puerta – lovely little vega running rich & deep
among the mountains – Almunecar blocking up the
entrance – valley cultivated with sugar – Diversified
by habitations – olives – Figs – oranges – aloes &c
&c – The old fortress stretches along the summit of

1. Salobreña, a town of about three or four thousand inhabitants,
on the coast some four miles from Motril, in the province of Granada.
2. On p. [98] Irving drew a sketch of a castle on the crest of a
mountain. At the bottom of p. [99] he appended a drawing of the
vega showing the position of the fishermen described on this page.
3. On p. [100] Irving drew a sketch of a battlemented town, perhaps
of Almuñécar. At the bottom of the drawing occurs the word "vega."
4. Almuñécar is a town of some four or five thousand inhabitants
in the province of Granada. It is on the coast some fifteen miles west
of Motril.

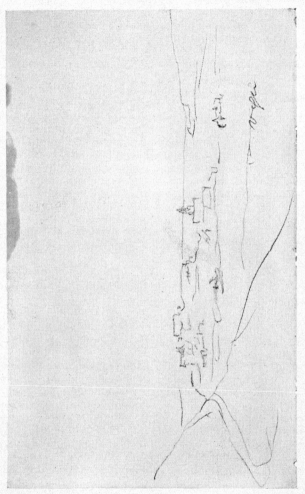

Irving's Sketch of a Town and Vega

hill [1] – two or three heights – towers – walls – battlements – Indian fig hangs over the Wall – aloes grow
at foot – repose of the delicious little vega in the
guardian embraces of mighty mountains – Blue Medi-
[102] [2] terranean in front – Soft climate – no harsh
weather – One of these little recesses on the stern
marble coast of the Mediterranean
Nevada the Mother of streams that water the kingdom of Granada
[103] Pass Sierras and at 12 oclock stop at a little
venta on the coast of the sea – on a bay embraced
by promontory – breakfast under shed in front of
cottage – The Bay is called Herradero [3] from its resemblance to a Horse shoe – afterwards wind up a
mountain through a deep rich glen clad with aromatic shrubs – Garcia sings songs of contrabandistas
– road passes along cornice of mount^s overhanging
the sea – which roars & breaks beneath – splendid
views along the coast – promontories – Lordly bold

1. Probably the fortress built by the command of Charles I, dominat-
ing the city and port with its four towers. It was blown up by the
English in 1812, and Irving refers, presumably, to the ruins.
2. At the top of this page Irving scribbled: "Indian fig hangs over its
ruined wall – blue Mediterranean – pear [?] and fig [?] – sugar
cane – watch tower – aqueduct."
3. This word refers to the act of branding cattle or to the place
where it is done. Probably Irving attempted to write *herradura*, the
word for horseshoe. A little village called Herradura, about four
miles from Almuñécar, probably takes its name from the bay.

style of scenery – Evening at 7 o clock arrive at
Nerja.[1] But one room to be had at the [104] posada &
that small damp and squalid – no fish – All in the
army – Stoffregen out of humour. Gessler & I begin
to eat cold hard eggs – Send Pepe to Alcayda [2] to
ask for his aid to procure beds – he comes to us – a
stout pleasant looking man procured us beds at a
friend – Our Landlady of the Posada bestirs her her-
self and gets us an excellent supper of Fish – Tomatoes
and rice & milk. Go to friend of Alcaldes – charming
corner with family & friends assembled led round it.
Smoke & chat and then return to room with al-
cove. Three clean beds in which we sleep luxuri-
ously.

[105] *Thursday 27* – In the morng our Landlord
brings morning drinks of Brandy – we bid farewell
of Alcalde in his shop & of our host & one or two
politicians who come to see us off –
– The vega in which Nerja is placed is pleasant with
sugar cane – We ride partly along the shore – partly
along Hills – One league of mountainous road – and
afterwards partly level –
– See a brig at sea – stop at sugar manufactory near

1. A town of about five thousand inhabitants, in the province of
Málaga, to the west of Almuñécar.
2. This word means jailer, warden, or governor of a castle, but
Irving probably attempted to write, as below, *Alcalde*, which means
mayor.

Toro [1] – arrive about 1 at Velez Malaga [2] – rich &
pleasing vega – grain – olives – &c. Velez on height
– old town – palm trees rising out of the town –
Mountains of various shapes some broken – rocky
– & others green – Country houses on the hills

[106] Velez Malaga – from the tower [3] Benamargosa[?] [4] to the east – Sierra tejada [5] to NE. valley
sloping to the sea river Velez running thro it –
valley rich with fields – country houses – citrons –
olives &c sea at distance –
Undulating mounts – with vast gray sierras at distance
Sometimes capd with clouds proportions[?] in Benamargosa – Other heights. Espando[?] & Cuenca[?]
Making snow river at one Christ[ian?] camp[?] [6]

1. Irving probably refers to Torrox, a town of about five thousand
inhabitants, in the province of Málaga, between Nerja and Vélez-
Málaga.
2. A town of about ten thousand inhabitants, in the province of
Málaga, about twenty miles from the city of Málaga.
3. Irving probably refers to the tower used as a lighthouse at Torre
del Mar, a village of about three thousand inhabitants some three
miles west of Vélez-Málaga, on the western bank of the Ménoba
River.
4. Irving's spelling for this word is very difficult to read, but it
appears certain that, in all three instances on this page of the Journal,
and in that on p. [108], he refers to *Benamargosa*, a town of about three
thousand inhabitants, some four miles from Vélez-Málaga. It is barely
possible that he wrote *Benamocarra*.
5. This is probably correct, but Irving possibly alludes to the Sierra
Tejea, a spur of which is very near Vélez-Málaga.
6. These two lines in the Journal are almost illegible.

Gullies between castle command city – Steep rocky side toward Benamargosa on the other side slopes down to river. with city between [107]¹ Old Moorish gateway in a street leading up to the castle – Public place part of the way up the hill –

We put up at Posada kept by a Frenchman – the best we have met with in Andalusia – good dinner – after dinner walk up to castle – see sunset – clouds gathering on mountain – afterwards descend & walk in small Patio & in the valley – town lies in lap of the Hill – with castle above it – miniature of Naples – Convent on rival Hill to the chateau –

On our return summoned by centinel to the commandant: Steffregen indignant scene with the commandant – our passports signed

[108] At night the Inn filled with people going from Granada to Malaga to pass Holy week – Like Canterbury pilgrims – women talking all the night

Friday 28. Bustle at Inn various parties going off – Women in saddles with sillas ² – Beautiful view of Velez – sun shining over Benamargosa – Gray Mountains of Sierra Tejada ³ – ride along the sea coast –

at 11 oclock – take breakfast of Fish at cabin at

1. At the top of this page Irving wrote: "Bausa Comand Militar a Velez Malaga."
2. The word *silla* itself means saddle. Irving probably refers to a high saddle or a sidesaddle, as used by women.
3. See p. 49, footnote 5.

foot of Rock – gypsey looking women – fish – sardaynes – Travellers passing – women – soldiers – command_ers – Horses at the shed – shed covrd with reeds – 13$\frac{1}{2}$ leagues from Malaga

[109] continue our ride along the coast sometimes under frowning rocks at others between hedges of Aloes – reeds &c – fishermen on shore drawing seines – road full of people – Houses with sheds coverd with vines – before them – Palm trees – resemblance to Italian scenes [1] – Turning a promontory we come in sight of Malaga – with its height of Gibralfaro [2] – Its blue waters and range of mountains stretching far beyond into the sea –

Put up at Hotel de la Europa – Deliver letter to Mr. Barrel [3] – our consul & pass part of the day walking with him.

[110] Saturday 29. Call this morng on Mr Barrel –

1. Irving traveled in Italy in 1805, and employed Italian settings for parts of *Tales of a Traveller* (1824). See S.T.W., I, 55–59.
2. The Gibralfaro hill, on the slopes of which are the older portions of Málaga. The Castle of Gibralfaro (in Arabic "mount of the beacon or lighthouse") affords an extensive view of the city and its suburbs, of the bay, and, at times, of the Melilla mountains, in Africa.
3. George G. Barrell, United States Consul at Málaga. For his associations with Irving, see S.T.W., I, 331, 483. The files of the American Consulate at Málaga have no record of Irving's visit, but contain considerable information concerning Barrell. Later files contain letters written to Barrell by Irving when he was Minister to Spain (1842–1846). *E.g.* Irving to G. G. Barrell, Madrid, November 14, 1842.

introduced by him to Mʳ Reed ¹ and to Mʳ Clervey deputy Am. Consul for Velez Malaga – walk up to Alcazaba ² – remains of Moorish arches – great corral in which the Moorish prisoners were confined –

Call with Stoffregen on Mʳ Ross Prussian consul – wife a lively pleasant woman – pretty daughter – some agreeable young men – one very well informed –

Dine at Mʳ Barrels present Mʳ Gessler & Stoffregen – Mr Reed – Col   ³ a Hanoverian Mʳ Clervey and the nephew of Mʳ Barrell –

[111] Evening – write a letter to Prince Dolgorouki ⁴ – but do not send it

Sunday 30 Sally forth at 6 oclock Mʳ Barrell sends a lad with me to show me Gibralfaro

Mount from the rear of the prison to the old fortress [112] Gibralfaro –

Cerro de Sᵗ Christoval ⁵ – where the marquis of Cadiz was situated

1. In the files of the American Consulate at Málaga, George Reed is described as a "resident merchant." From a document headed Málaga, February 14, 1829, and signed by Reed, who was attached in some capacity to the Consulate. During Irving's stay in Madrid as minister, Reed was consul at Málaga. *E.g.*, Irving to George Reed, Madrid, July 31, 1843 (Files of the American Consulate, Málaga).

2. Moorish fortress or citadel, whose ruins are now occupied chiefly by gypsies.

3. Irving's blank.

4. For Irving's friendship with the Russian Prince Dolgorouki, see S.T.W., I, 358–362, and *passim*.

5. The Hill of St. Christopher, between Gibralfaro and Calvario.

– next mount Calvary [1]

convent of La Victoria at the foot of Calvary

dry bed of the River Guadalmedina [2] –

Deep wall in fortress – Massive walls – weeds – nettles & thistles among aromatic herbs

Hill of Gibralfaro cultivated with vines – Indian figs

View from Gibralfaro down into the city squares of convents – Palm trees Plaza de Merced [3] – Plazauela de la Victoria [4] – Vega surrounded by Mounts snowy heights of Mija [5] in the [115] distance

[116] [6] In the time of rain the Guadalmedina fills its dry bed and comes roaring down from the bosom of the wild mountains

Hamed [7] from the tower could discern the commanders prancing in the valleys below him.

1. Monte Calvario.
2. This river runs through the city of Málaga, dividing it into two unequal parts.
3. The Plaza de la Merced is near the center of the city, a little to the east.
4. The Plaza de la Victoria is in the northeastern part of the city.
5. The Sierra de Mijas or Sierra Blanca, which runs parallel to the coast and reaches a height of about thirty-five hundred feet.
6. Following p. [112] is merely the fragment of a leaf torn out, pp. [113, 114]. P. [115] is blank except for the single word in the upper left hand corner: "distance." Regular entries in the Journal recommence on p. [116].
7. The Moorish chief of Málaga, Hamed-Zegrí, who shut himself up in the tower of the Gibralfaro during the siege of Málaga (1487), and refused to surrender until twenty-four hours after the city was captured. See *The Conquest of Granada*, pp. 355–378.

Wild line of rocky mount^s that bound the distances –
misty levels –

Morng sun shining along the eastern coast – glittering
beyond the promontories – blue sea scarce united by
a bridge

Camp drawn so nigh the city that the tent of [117]
each commander could be discerned

In the courts of Gibralfaro where the weed and wild
flower mingle & grass grows over the crumbling
tower

Broken heights that approach the tower – Steep
towards the sea

Fine view of Malaga from road to Colmenar [1]

[118] Convent of Trinidad [2] on a mound fronting
the centre of Malaga – The rear guard of the Kings
army

Dine at Mr Reed's present Mr Gessler – Stoffregen
– M^r. Rand & nephew – Col Newman – M^r. Clervey
– evening M^r.   [3] comes in

Afterwards go to private concert at   [4]

[119] Monday March 31. Breakfast with Mr Barrell

---

1. A town of about four thousand inhabitants some eighteen miles
north of Málaga.
2. The Convento de la Trinidad, founded on a site occupied by a
hermitage. This was erected in 1487 by General Francisco Ramírez
in honor of Saint Onofre. Tradition says that the saint counseled
the general through dreams how best to vanquish the Moors.
3. Irving's blank.
4. Irving's blank.

afterwards drive out into the country with the family of the Rosses – visit the Retiro [1] – seat of Count de Valles [?] Casa called the Versailles of Malaga dine at Mr Rosses country seat – visit seat of great —— —— [2]

Evg at concert at Lopez the Bass singer – Hear fine singing from ——

[120] April 1. Breakfast with Barrell – call with him on Col Breman[?], who takes us to S^t [3] descendant of Count Tendilla – Has the sword & dagger of his ancestor –

Dine with Mr Barrell – evg walk out to the coast – M^r. Plowes [4]

[121] April 2. Breakfast with Barrell write letters – call on Russian consul M^r.   [5]

Dine at Mr Barrells – M^r. Plowes Send letters to M^{le} Bolviller [6] – Prince Dolgorouki [7] – Mr Wilkie [8] Get 40 Dollars of Crocker & Brothers – Bankers –

1. El Retiro is an estate about three miles from the city, later the property of the Marquis of Puerto Seguro.
2. Four words are illegible.
3. Irving's blank.
4. John E. Plowes, American Vice Consul (Files of the American Consulate, Málaga).
5. Irving's blank.
6. An intimate friend in Madrid, to whom Irving wrote some of his most delightful letters descriptive of Spain. See S.T.W., Index.
7. See *idem*, I, 358–362; 481–482; and *passim*.
8. For Irving's friendship with David Wilkie, the English painter, see *idem*, I, 333–336, and *passim*.

[122] April 3. Thursday. Leave Malaga $\frac{1}{2}$ past 6 – cross the river of Guadalmedina – we have two gens D'armes one mounted, the other on foot – and a boy with a carbine – pass flock of sheep on road – conducted by men armed with muskets – See Cartama [1] to our left – on slope of hill – ruined castle above on rocky height – beyond Alaurin [2] – surrounded by trees – vega widens before them – rocky and mountains – those of the Hungera [?] [3] with snow on them – at $\frac{1}{2}$ past 10 stop at Venta by the road side called Venta de Alhama – take second breakfast

[123] Venta – Long stable of a house – supported by 4 Brick columns – roof smoked – muleteer or traveller lying on his brown capa on round stones at door – pillow under his head – cartridge box – spurs – Leather gaiters –

Mules coming in with cantaros [4] of water – table two feet high – Men seated under fig trees & aloes behind house eating oranges – Gens darmes – smoking &c

Steep & toilsome ride up the mountain – pass village of Alosina [5] – wild & zigzag road through a pass which opens to the west – beautiful [124] pros-

---

1. A small town of about four thousand inhabitants, west of Málaga.
2. I have been unable to identify this place. Irving may possibly refer to Alahurín de la Torre or Alahurín al Granada.
3. I have been unable to identify this place. Irving may possibly refer to Junquera.   4. Jugs, or pitchers.
5. Alozaina, a town of about three thousand people.

pect – valley among steep rocks – road passes through narrow puerto & winds along precipices called Puerto of Herrez [?] [1] – Here the french lost many men by an ambuscade – Put up for the night at the village of Jungura [2] – in the high parts of the mountains – burying ground on a height commanding view over valley of Malaga

See Coin [3] in the distance showers of rain during this afternoons ride

[125] At the Inn we sit in the chimney corner – with Gens D'armes – muleteers &c – other part of the Hall is the stable

– Landlord a tall wiry dark good looking man – pretty daughter big with child – a young girl of 13 also very pretty – a handsome tall young man for his son – We have a room about 10 feet square allotted us – three great pieces of new[?] brown cloth for beds – sit on the cloth & sup off of a low table or stool – a large brown bowl of boiled milk & bread – we all three eat out of the same dish – eggs – &c –

Rain in the night – go out of the room – Muleteers & guards sleeping about the stable and the hearth – wrapped in their cloaks and lying on the stones –

[126] April 4. Good Friday – rainy morning – Leave

1. Probably Puerto Jerez, some forty miles from Granada.
2. Irving refers to the mountain village of Junquera.
3. Coín is a town of some ten thousand inhabitants in the province of Málaga, some twenty-five miles from the city of Málaga.

our Posada at about 7. Ascend the mountains of Junquera to Burgo [1] – situated among mountains with verdant fields around it remains of old walls – clouds drifting about the mountains – Cuesta de Burgos [2] – steep slippery – miry – after ascending it we have a little good road & then come to Los dientes de la Vieja [3] lime stone ridge – difficult descent – From this place we have a prospect back towards Malaga –

Passing the heights of Junquera [4] we descend a little into the plain above Ronda – Oak trees vineyards – olives – arrive at Ronda ½ past 2 – 4 leagues this day – Fine view from the Alameda [5] –
walk about the streets – beautiful women – fine men dressed es majo *Perdona Vida* [6]

[127] Bridge of Ronda unites two precipices – a deep ravine which separates the two parts of town – Indian fig – aloes – Dark green weeds – swallows

1. A town of about three thousand inhabitants, some ten miles from Ronda.
2. Hill of Burgo.
3. The Old Woman's Teeth.
4. The Sierra de la Junquera is in the province of Málaga.
5. The Alameda, or Paseo de la Merced, is near the edge of the gorge through which flows, about six hundred feet below, the Guadalevín River. This ravine separates the old and new parts of the city. Ronda held a fascination for Irving almost equal to that of Granada.
6. Spanish phrases which Irving may have heard as he walked about the city. *Es majo:* is showily dressed. *Perdonavidas:* bully or braggart.

skim[in]g – roar of water – Well – old Moorish house casa del rey [1] – Houses & little garden backg on ravine – rocks like towers & bastions

Hurrying mist & rain from mountains – watery gleam of sunshine

Pillo – a Coquin [2]

Perdona Vida – A man wrapped in mantle with knife –

Heights of Grasalema [3] & Cortes [4] the latter very peaked the former seen on coming from America

[129] [5] April 5 – Saturday – Last night stormy – wind rain – Look out from window – beautiful effect of moonlight breaking through mist – on Bridge & white houses along the bank of the river ravine & white houses & colonades of square – walk out at 6 – descend below the bridge narrow zig zag road cut thro rocks – small Moorish gateway half way down –

1. The Casa del Rey Moro, built, tradition says, during the reign of Abumelek. Beneath this is a huge subterranean vault, probably used by the Moors as reservoirs of water during sieges.
2. *Pillo* means rascal, and Irving noted also the French equivalent.
3. Grazalema is a county and town in the province of Cádiz, about fifty miles from the city of Cádiz. In this very mountainous country one peak, Cerro de San Cristóbal is more than five thousand feet in height.
4. Irving probably refers to a township called Cortes de la Frontera on the slope of the Sierra de Líbar, southwest of Ronda, and in the province of Málaga.
5. On p. [128] Irving drew a sketch of the bridge and gorge of Ronda.

waterfalls below bridge – water gushing thro arches of bridge – aloes – wet weeds hanging down over rocks –

Old town built along crest ,of height – rocks of pudding stone like bastions –
In streets pass frequent crosses – here was killed the unfortunate Don ——— [1] pray God for his soul –
[130] In Ronda – fine Careo[?] de Toros [2] very large – two stages
Banks of river hung with Indian figs – aloes &c
Great square – Men with oranges for sale – of great size & beauty – Piles of fine bread – Droves of black sheep & lambs –

Majos – Brown cloak with green or crimson velvet – Breeches of mulberry or brown – or green – embroidered with black – gilt buttons – sashes red – yellow or white – Jackets with crimson velvet at sleeves – gilt hangs & buttons – Vest open – ruffled – shirt – sometimes col^d handkf under hat
[131] Leave Ronda ¼ past 8. Rain – we are told by man on Donkey to be cautious as he had seen suspicious people on the road – just after this we ascend

1. Irving's dash.
2. The first word in this Spanish phrase is difficult to decipher. It may be *Casa*. Irving refers to the Plaza de Toros, which is said to be the oldest in Spain (1784). An unusual feature of its construction is that seats in both the lower and upper parts of the stadium have roofs with supporting columns.

steep & rugged pass – the Cuesta de Arrebata Capa [1]
– At the entrance a cross – Solitary roads – turns
among rocks – wild mountain scenery – distant view
of Ronda – cloud of mist comes scouring thro deep
defile – road winds along precipices – we are wrapped
in mist – Afterward sunshine – wild broken mount
scenery – checquered with mist – gleams of sunshine
– green spots & shelves of mountain – olive trees –
rain – Bright view from mountain road – floating sea
of clouds – rocks – valleys below – green hills – stop
at village of Atahate [2]
while horse shod get eggs & in a cottage
[132] Mountains, with clouds – pass four men with
two mules – 4 escopetas suspicious looking fellows –
turn out to be justice of village & his followers who
had conducted a robber to prison – Excessively rough
passes – ride wrapped in cloak – with rain & mist
past the village of Benlaure[?] [3] below with Old castle
on promontory – convent hermitage with cypress –
    Beautiful mountain rides – looking down on vil-
lages – far below – like from clouds. – See [4]

---

1. Irving speaks here of Puerto (mountain pass) de Arrebata-capas,
situated between Ronda and Gaucín. *Arrebata-capas* means literally:
snatches capes, or cape-snatcher, or robber.
2. Irving refers to Atajate, a village of about four hundred people.
3. Irving probably alludes to Benelauria, north of Gaucín.
4. After "See" Irving crossed out the phrase "villages below us."
At the bottom of this page [132] he wrote: "Lying on the side of a

[133] At a pass of the mountain suddenly come upon the valley of Algaussin [1] magical scene – valleys with trees – oaks – great towering height of Casare [2] the hight of Algaussin with old castle of Moors & Romans – valley fresh enameled – clouds driving about it – cloud sun often like the curtain of theater

Rock of castle is called el Tajo del nino de Dios [3] – many sculls & bones of Moors have been found there – many of various kinds – The castle breaks out from among clouds & mist towering high in the air

We have passed mountains covered with vine-yards

---

hill on Summer day musing with half shut eye on the wide plain – glimmering with sunshine." The regular entries in the Journal are resumed on p. [133].

1. It is almost certain that Irving refers here and later to the site of Gaucín, a town of about thirty-five hundred inhabitants, in the extreme southwestern part of the province of Málaga. This is one of the most picturesque places in all Andalusia. Presumably the "Al" is merely the Arabic definite article, and the "ss" is used instead of "c."

2. Although Irving omitted the final "s," it is certain that here he alludes to the height of Casares, a prominent peak in this region. There is also a town of Casares about twelve miles from Gaucín, and situated on this height. The two parallel ridges which form the spine of the Serranía de Ronda begin, respectively, in the vicinity of Gaucín and Casares.

3. On the heights above Gaucín are the ruins of a Moorish castle (destroyed by an explosion fifteen years after Irving's visit). The town is situated on the edge of a deep gorge (tajo). The name which Irving here applies to the rocky height is probably that of the gorge. In or near the town is a hermitage called "Ermita del Niño Dios."

[134] Spanish Posada – fireplace seats in it – Pucheros [1] ranged above – lamp hanging to it earthen floor – Blind man in corner – Gossips of village coming in – roof smoked – rows of brown earthen dishes – cupboard in niche of wall – rest of house paved – eye lost in distance – Stables dimly lighted with lamps

This day we have been from $\frac{1}{4}$ past 8 in morning until $\frac{1}{2}$ past 5 making five leagues –

This day past in sight of Cortes [2] to the right – in this place the french have never entered [3]

[135] pass the night at the posada del sol – good people – we have three rooms – beds on floor but clean – Landladys daughter Marujita [Margarita?]

view from my window between mount covered with vineyards into a deep woody valley – Blue mountain in distance covered with clouds.

April 6 Leave Algaussin at 6 o'clock grand view descending – effect of sun effulgent gleam. from among clouds down a dark green valley –

Point of view from hill about a mile from Algausin the range of Sierra de Ronda – view south along a

1. Earthen pots used for cooking.
2. Cortes de la Frontera, a town of about twenty-five hundred inhabitants, in the county of Gaucín, and in the province of Málaga.
3. Probably a boast which Irving heard from these people, who never ceased from their relentless guerrilla warfare during the War of Independence.

valley with river gleamg toward the sea – to left a deep valley with high mounts – to right Sierra Himera [1] steep [136] almost conical – rocky – cross on height – treasures of Moors on this mount –

turn behind – Algausin on ridge of mount – Convent – rugged point of tajo nino de Dios with towers of old Moorish castle – Slight Shower – rainbow –

Scenery broken with mountains – Steep and difficult descent for nearly a league – arrive at the bed of the river –

Plantation of oranges & citrons there – Superb orange trees laden with fruit & flowers – ride along the bed of the river for a couple of leagues – cross it several times – Have various views of Algausin – Take a repast in the shelter of a laurel bush on the banks of the river – Quarrel between our escort & some Dependientes [2] at a Venta about a dog –

[137] We have rain in the course of the day – ride along the Sea shore – distant view of Gibraltar – coverd with clouds – Sea coast – gulls – deep sand – Arrive at Spanish lines about 5 o'clock – Difficulty about examining our luggage – pay a trifle & pass – Are stopped at lines of Gibraltar – Have to send our passports to our consuls – fearful of being detained

---

1. Probably Irving's spelling for Jimera. The village of Jimera de Líbar is about twelve miles from Gaucín.
2. Employees, or servants.

until after the hour of closing gates – Send in my card
to the commanding officer & a tall handsome young
officer comes out and immediately suffers us to pass –
Put up at Hotel Mahomett – visit from Mr Sprague [1]

1. For Irving's friendship with the Spragues, who were, for more
than a hundred years, associated with the American Consulate at
Gibraltar, see S.T.W., I, 332, 368, 483, 498.

At this point in the Journal, the formal entries end, on April 6,
1828, when Irving arrived at Gibraltar. Irving resumed his record
on April 7, 1828 in another volume, already published as *Washington
Irving, Diary, Spain, 1828–1829*, ed. C. L. Penney, New York, 1926.

The remainder of the present volume is concerned with memo-
randa made at various times along the route, and especially in
Granada. See Introduction. After the entry concerning Mr. Sprague
were written the passages which I have called "Miscellaneous Notes
on Moorish Legend and History." These notes have no known chron-
ological sequence and they have, therefore, for the sake of clarity, been
rearranged. While keeping the Journal, Irving at intervals turned the
book upside down, and set down these observations, whenever they
occurred to him, working from the back of the book toward the
front. The pages on which these entries appear are indicated by the
figures in brackets.

MISCELLANEOUS NOTES

ON

MOORISH LEGEND AND HISTORY

MISCELLANEOUS NOTES

[137] Alonso D Aguilar [1] – His sword sent to Hanover –

Sword[?] ages[?] in family – When the french came & the city was disarmed the family threw it in a well – at the end of two years it was got out – Spoiled —

[139] About 30 years since an invalid had charge of the Alhambra to show it. He was a poor man, with a large family. As he was one evening about twilight in the court of the Lions he saw in the great Hall to the right, four Moors richly Dressed & armed walking to & fro. They called to him but he was so frightened that he ran off, and would never return to the Alhambra. Misfortune fell upon him. He died not long after & his family went to ruin. His successor was more fortunate. He entered the Alhambra poor, but in three months he left it rich: went to Velez Malaga bought Spaniard clothes & lives there yet very rich – How he came by his wealth no one knows. Supposed to have been informed by the 4 Moors where their money was hid.[2]

[138] Aljebello[?] Walk along the Darro

1. Alonso de Aguilar, a Spanish nobleman and warrior who was killed by the Moors in the Sierra Bermeja (January, 1501) during a rebellion caused by a decree ordering all Mohammedans to be baptized.
2. See *The Alhambra*, "The Adventure of the Mason" and the "Legend of the Moor's Legacy."

Fuente de Avellano.[1]

Los Culebrones de Gracia [2] Shut up in the marble bosom of the Alpuxarras

[141] Torre de los pico [3] – Himenes [4] father had garden & flowergarden there – Say that his father told him that in old times it was inhabited by an invalid one of the guard – When about at night his wife heard noise – a giant stood before her – She exclaimed – her husband came – told him of the giant Moor – He saw nothing – the next night her husband busy on guard – the giant appeared – Said he not affraid – speak to me – She demanded what do you want – Under this tower is a treasure buried – take it & enjoy it as long as you live – When her husband returned she recounted it – He searched – found bricks & removed them – opend a cave – Skeleton of two [140] Moors with armour – pikes &c box of iron with 3 Keys – great store of gold – purchased a mule & made off – 14 years afterward his son came & dispensed alms accordg to the direction of his father to various of the inhabitants.

1. These and the adjacent phrases are evidently jottings made during Irving's stay in Granada. Aljebello[?] I have been unable to identify. The famous Fuente del Avellano is situated a short distance from Granada, near the Darro River.
2. The origin of this phrase I have been unable to identify. *Culebrones* means large snakes; cunning fellows, or "snakes in the grass."
3. Irving refers to the Torre de los Picos, a tower of the Alhambra.
4. Mateo Ximénez. See p. 21, footnote 3.

[143] The tower from whence Chiquito [1] sallied had 7 stages underground – The old people of the Alhambra say that a horse without a head used to sally forth at midnight with Seven dogs & Scour the city frightening all the inhabitants & returning at break of day tradition says that a Moorish governor of the Alhambra had slain 7 men[?] & buried them in the cavern of this tower

No one could go lower than 4 of the stories as there was such a wind as to extinguish the light – Ximenes [2] tells stories told him by his grandfather who was 93 years of age & died 7 years since. His father still lives & is 70 – he is 35 – was born in the Alhambra & has always lived here, excepting 2 years that the [142] French were here [3]

girl at night saw Moorish pageant in hall – Shadowy court of Boabdil – procession seen by Moonlight going from the tower whence Boabdil issued

[146] – Matteo Ximenes says that there was much treasure buried by the Moors – thinking that they would return & not having much time to carry off

1. See p. 19, footnote 3.
2. See S.T.W., Chap. XV, *passim*.
3. The French occupied Granada from 1810 to 1812, and later from 1820 to 1822. During their second stay they attempted to blow up the Alhambra, thus destroying the Torre de Siete Suelos and other parts of the structure.

these things (doubtless at time of banishment) – One
Moor made a cave put all his treasure there and left
an enchanted man to guard it – an hundred years
passed away – The inhabitants of the house be-
gan to see apparitions – hear clanking of chains –
Consult a Moor turned christian – He has a book
in Arabic characters – tells the way to recover enchanted treasure – they must read prayers at midnight – When the earth trembles they must light a
taper of yellow wax – If the light is extinguished
before they get out the treasure they will remain enchanted – The [145] men at midnight read prayer –
& dig – earth trembles – they are frightened and fly.
Second night they read – earthquake – light candle
– read – opens wall – find within a man seated on a
box – armed with lance &c – get the gold divide it
among themselves – Moor goes to Portugal – one of
the men to Gibraltar – the other to France –
Others have not been so fortunate – find bull with
treasure who attacks them – one reveals his luck to
the corregidor [1] who takes it all from him
[147] [2] The tower of the center corner[?] – about
60 years since inhabited by a man – woman &
daughter who wove ribbands – time of distress –

1. *Corregidor:* mayor, or magistrate.
2. At the bottom of this page, written upside down, is the word
"Generalife."

nothg to eat – parents absent – child at work late at
night – door opens – Man enters walks up & down –
child at work – Do not fear – what have you for
supper – points out mans supper[?] – afterwards says
since you have not cried & in proportion to your
courage shall be your reward – take this – kicked
toward her a skin of wine – Her father came home –
she recounted the story – the skin full of gold – the
man got a mule next day put his bag of gold on it &
pushed off

[150] Torre de los Infantas [1] – The tower was given
by the Governor of the Alhambra to be inhabited by
a poor family – one night a woman was washing
clothes at a small marble fountain – water trembles –
figure of a Moorish princess rises – Be not frightned –
lighten[?] me, then I may have rest – I have on my
head enough to buy half Granada – The woman very
frightnd & her Sister ran down – figure disappeared
– Second night the two sisters – The figure again
appeard – They threw water – the figure disappeared
& the fountain [149] remained full of gold – The
day after they get the gold – pushed off & with them
brother & have never since been heard of –

[148] Torre del Agua – in ruins [2]

1. Torre de los Infantes. See p. 24, footnote 4.
2. One of the Alhambra's ruined towers, of which Irving appends
a sketch, with the word "Ivy."

[144] Houses about Granada rent by earthquakes
– but Alhambra still stands [1]

[155] [2] Torre de los infantes inhabited – remains of
arabesques &c

Torre de los Captivos [3]

[156] Andarax [4] & the Salinas [5] of Malcha[?] – given
to El Zagal [6] the Moorish King

Purchena [7] to Chiquito

– Fez Alla Aibar – not far from Padul [8] – the ultimo
suspiro del Moro

Alcazaba fortress in the Albaycin

Convent of St Ieronimo – the marble chair of Gonzalo Fernandez

Plaza de Vivarrambla [9]

Standards of Gonzalo Fernandez of Cordova in Convent of St Jeronimo [10]

1. The rest of this page is devoted to a sketch of part of the Alhambra.
2. Pp. [151, 152] are blank. Pp. [153, 154] form a leaf which, except for a small fragment, is torn out.
3. Irving refers to the Torre de la Cautiva. See p. 32, footnote 2.
4. The name of a district or region in the kingdom of Granada.
5. *Salinas:* salt mines.
6. El Zagal was Chiquito's uncle, and his bitter rival for the
control of Granada. See *The Conquest of Granada*, p. 87 ff.
7. Purchena is a town of about two thousand inhabitants in the
province of Almería.
8. See p. 34, footnote 4.
9. The Bibarrambla, one of the principal squares of Granada, where
tourneys were held.
10. Another reference to the Gran Capitán, who was buried in the
church of this convent of St. Jerónimo.

[157] Road to the Summit of the Hill of Martyrs [1] – where it led to the gate of the mills opposite to the Alhambra – The cardinal [2] dispatched his comitiva[?] [3] to take possession of the red tower [4] & the tower of the gate of Gomeres [5] then ascending the tower of the Vela [6] he elevated on its Summit the standard of Spain &c

Procession from the camp came to village of Armilla ½ league from city

– procession moved forward to hermitage of St. Sebastian on banks of Xenil where the Moorish King paid homage & surrendd keys.

Huerta del rey – where the Duke of Infantado [7] & Bishop Ossorio

[158] Ojos de Huescar [8] 1 & ½ leagues from Granada – where Ferdinand encamped –

1. See p. 23.   2. Cardinal Mendoza.
3. This word is difficult to decipher. Irving probably wrote *comitiva*, retinue or followers; or he may have written chambers, as an abbreviation for chamberlains.
4. Irving refers to the Torres Bermejas.
5. The name of the street which leads to the Puerta de las Granadas, a modern gate.
6. When the Spaniards took possession of the Alhambra on January 12, 1492, the cross of the cardinal and the standards of Santiago and of Ferdinand were placed on the Torre de la Vela.
7. The Duque del Infantado, Diego Hurtado de Mendoza. The official title created by Ferdinand and Isabella in 1475 was "duque de las Cinco Villas del Estado del Infantado."
8. *Ojos:* eyes. Cf. p. 77. There is a town called Huéscar in the extreme northern part of the province of Granada.

Alcazaba & the red towers

Valley of Linden

Hamlet of Zubia near to the city – from whence the Queen saw the fight – To commemorate it she afterwards erected a monastary in Zubia – dedicated it to St Francisco

Castle of Roma – 2 Leagues

Tower & town of Alhendin [1] near Alpuxarras – town overthrown by the Moors

[159]   Moclin [2] – Shield of Granada – miraculous explosion of a tower

Solemn entry Te deum

Castle of Roma two leagues from Granada – town[?] taken by Cabra[?] [3]

Alcala [4] – Count Tendilla [5] had town built on height in neighborhood

1. See p. 23, footnote 5.

2. A town of about four thousand inhabitants north of Granada. During its possession by the Moors its powerful fortress defended the frontier north of the city, for which reason it was called "Escudo de Granada" or "Shield of Granada." At Moclín the Christians were defeated in 1485, but they conquered the town in the following year.

3. Probably Diego Fernández de Córdoba, the Count of Cabra, who, with the Count of Tendilla, was active in attacking Moorish strongholds near Granada.

4. Probably Alcalá la Real, a township of about fifteen thousand inhabitants located in the extreme southern part of the province of Jaén. The town itself has a population of about six thousand. See also p. 16, footnote 3.

5. See *The Conquest of Granada,* pp. 182 ff.

Hears one day that the Moors had made a sally towards Quesada [1] – lays in ambush near Barzena [2] Adra [3] surprised by vessel filled with X^n disguised as Moors.

[161] Illora [4] – a strong tower perched on a high rock in the midst of a spacious valley – It was fortified with walls & towers & its lofty castle com[an]d^d a great circuit of country – it was called the right eye of Granada – It is only 4 leagues from the metropolis

King fixed camp on the hill of Encinilla – rest of the army stationed about the city – fortified camp with branches & pallisades

Duke of Infantado demands the attack – (having been reproached with foray of his troops)

Christ[ian]s take suburbs – Duke one suburb Count of Cabra another – assailed wall of town with lombard for a couple of days

– Great havoc towers overthrown houses demolished – such a din the Moors could not hear each other

1. A town of about fifty-five hundred inhabitants in the eastern part of the province of Jaén.
2. This place I have been unable to identify.
3. Mediterranean seaport of about sixty-five hundred inhabitants in the province of Almería. Boabdil el Chico was permitted to live here for two years before withdrawing to Africa.
4. A town of about four thousand inhabitants in the province of Granada about thirty-five miles northwest of the city. The Moors called its fortress "El ojo de Granada."

speak – no room to fight – steep [160] place makes
signal to surrender – Inhabitants permitted to depart
& are escorted by Duke of Infant [1] to the puente
del Pinos [2] – place repaird & left in charge of Gon-
sales of Cordova Capt of royal guards of Ferd &
Isab.[3]

Moors intendg to defend the place to the last had
sent their women & chi[l]d[ren] & aged to Granada – Barricaded the suburbs – opened doors of
communication from house to house & pierced the
walls of the houses with loop holes

One of the Brothers alcayde [4] of Illora – the other
of Moclin [5]

After capture of Illora King moves camp to Moclin
where he is visited by Isabela [6]

[163] Las Ciudades no pueden traer Estandartes
Quadrados sino haspados, y solo los Reyes y Em-
peradores los pueden traer quadrados –

N. Reynoso Hist Ronda
MS [7]

1. Irving's abbreviation for Infantado.
2. Irving refers to the town of Pinos-Puente, six miles from Illora.
3. See *The Conquest of Granada*, p. 282.
4. Governor of a fortress.
5. See p. 76, footnote 2.
6. See *The Conquest of Granada*, pp. 284–289.
7. This passage reads in English: The cities may not carry square
standards but in the form of a cross, and only the kings and emperors
may carry them square.

[162] Cabra – Baena – Lucena [1]
defeated at Moclin [2] – the shield of Granada
What distance is Baena from Lucena – the inter-
vening mountains of Hirquera – defile which leads
to Lucena
  Don Diego Hernandez de Cordova Alcayde de los
Donceles [3]
  King Chiquito taken near the riverlet Mingon-
zales [4]
Aliasen[?] overtaken & slain on the banks of the
Xenil
[164] [5] —— —— [6] Relaziones curiosas de la Biblioteca Episcopal de Cordova recogidas por el conde
de Miranda

1. Cabra (population 13,000), Baena (population 13,000), and
Lucena (population 18,000), are towns in the province of Cordova.
2. Preceding "defeated" Irving crossed out a word, presumably
an abbreviation of "Christians." The Christians were defeated here
in 1485.
3. Hernandez is Irving's name for Fernández. Diego Fernández de
Córdoba was "alcaide de los Donceles." The *donceles* were youths of
noble rank who, after serving as pages to the King, were enrolled in a
picked militia commanded by a chief called the *alcaide*.
  Diego Fernández de Córdoba, a native of Lucena and governor
of the city, was besieged there by a Moorish army led by Boabdil
himself. On April 23, 1483 Fernández raised the siege and cleverly
outwitted the Moors, carrying the battle to the plain of Martín
González. Here the Christians won an overwhelming victory, and
Boabdil el Chiquito was taken prisoner. See Irving's use of these
episodes in *The Conquest of Granada*, pp. 598–621.
4. Probably an abbreviation of the name of the field of battle,
Martín González.   5 and 6. See next page for notes.

Padre Roa – arch[bishop?] of Malaga
– Conversaciones malagenas by Sancho ——
Hist de Ronda Por N Reynoso

[FINIS]

5. This is the last page in the volume, except the covers, on which writing occurs. The last leaf, forming pp. [165, 166] is torn out. On the right hand inside cover are written the following notes:

          2 camisas
          5 corbatas
          2 panuelos de Batista
          1 —— [Irving's dash] de Seda
          3 cuellos
          1 chaleco
          1 p. calcetines

Also, upside down:

          Almunecar receivd at ——
          Cartama
          Alora
          Coyn
          35
          el tajo del Calderero

6. Three words are illegible.

ADDENDUM

Attention is called to Irving's mention, on pages 14 and 43, of the murder of travelers. This is shocking brutality, but it must be remembered that such incidents occurred in the Spain of more than a century ago, and not in the serene, civilized Spain of our own age.

Thus one is tempted to be ironical. Or mildly philosophical. Whither Spain?

Yet those who love Spain know that she is great, greater even than her tragedy of today. The peace of those older days will return!

1 June, 1937   S.T.W.